ARTHRITIS

The Essential Guide

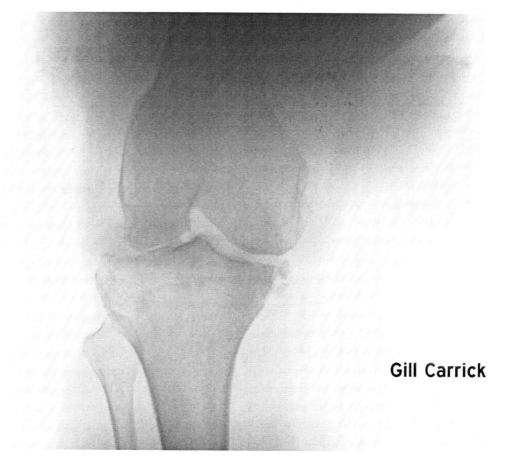

Gill Carrick

Arthritis – The Essential Guide is also available in accessible formats for people with any degree of visual impairment. The large print edition and eBook (with accessibility features enabled) are available from Need2Know. Please let us know if there are any special features you require and we will do our best to accommodate your needs.

First published in Great Britain in 2011 by
Need2Know
Remus House
Coltsfoot Drive
Peterborough
PE2 9BF
Telephone 01733 898103
Fax 01733 313524
www.need2knowbooks.co.uk

All Rights Reserved
© Gill Carrick 2011
SB ISBN 978-1-86144-131-7
Cover photograph: Dreamstime

Contents

EDINBURGH LIBRARIES	
C0044427956	
Bertrams	15/08/2011
	£9.99
DVHQ	RC933

This book is dedicated to the memory of my parents, Robert and Mary Elliott, who were both affected by arthritis. My mother suffered from Polymyalgia Rheumatica (PMR) and coped with fortitude. My father had severe osteoarthritis in his right knee and carried on regardless. I'm sure both would be heartened by the recent progress made in the care for others with this disease.

Introduction

If you've been diagnosed with arthritis, it's understandable you might have concerns and questions you'd like answered and hopefully this guide will go some way to addressing these.

Packed with practical advice; information on the latest treatments; first-hand experiences; expert opinions and coping mechanisms, the guide aims to help you stay positive and effectively manage your own condition.

Arthritis affects around 10 million people in the UK - including 12,000 children under the age of 16 - and accounts for one in five visits to a GP. As there are so many different forms of arthritis, including over 100 inflammatory and rheumatic conditions, not all of them can be covered in this guide. So the focus will be on the main types of arthritis, including osteoarthritis, the most common form, and autoimmune disorders such as rheumatoid arthritis and lupus.

Being given a diagnosis of arthritis can be daunting, yet with new treatments underway and efforts to find a cure, there is every reason to stay optimistic and not let arthritis control your life. Joining forums – most of the arthritis charities and organisations have them on their websites – and local support groups, is a great way to swap experiences and help you feel you're not alone.

While the standards of care for people with arthritis are getting better all the time, the situation isn't perfect. So if you think there's room for improvement in your own case, or that of a family member, discuss this with your doctor - and push if you have to!

Finally, remember there is life after an arthritis diagnosis. It's just part of who you are, not all of you.

Disclaimer

This book provides general information only, and is not intended in any way as a substitute for the medical advice of your own GP, consultant or any other healthcare professional. Always consult your own doctor if you are in any way concerned that you or a family member might have arthritis, and need advice or a referral to a consultant.

It is important to check with your GP or healthcare professional before acting on any of the information given in this guide, as recommendations might change and new treatments are being developed all the time.

All the information provided in this book was correct at time of going to press and no responsibility can be taken for any omission or error.

Chapter One

Osteoarthritis (OA)

Osteoarthritis is the most common form of arthritis, with around 8 million men and women in the UK suffering from the condition. Known as the 'wear and tear' disease, osteoarthritis affects almost everyone over 40 in some way, although younger people and children can develop it too. Women are more susceptible to the condition than men.

While several different joints can be affected, osteoarthritis is seen most frequently in the hands, knees, hips, feet and spine.

What is osteoarthritis?

Osteoarthritis is the slow destruction of the joint by wear and tear as we age and our body's ability to repair itself declines. To understand osteoarthritis, it's perhaps helpful to look at how joints work.

Synovial joint

The correct term for the type of joint in which arthritis can develop, is a 'synovial joint'. A synovial joint consists of two or more bones in contact with each other, and able to move against each other. Synovial joints can be described in terms of their movements. For example:

- Hinge joints – in the knee and elbow
- Ball and socket joints – in the hip and shoulder

The joint is enclosed by a tough capsule which is lined with a layer of synovial membrane which secretes lubricant fluid and provides nourishment to the tissue within the joint.

'Osteoarthritis is the most common form of arthritis, with around 8 million men and women in the UK suffering from the condition.'

Ligaments

Thickened parts of the capsule, called ligaments, help control movement. There might also be ligaments lying separate from the capsule. The knee, for example, has tough collateral ligaments on both sides which allow it to bend and straighten, but which prevent it from bending sideways. If a strong enough force is applied to bend the knee sideways, as happens when a football or rugby player is tackled from the side, or in skiing accidents, the ligament could rupture.

There are also strong ligaments running through the middle of the knee called cruciate (crossover) ligaments. Their job is to prevent the lower bone (tibia) from sliding too far forwards or backwards under the upper bone (femur).

Cartilage

All the surfaces within a joint which can make contact, are covered with a material that is 20 times more slippery than ice. This is called hyaline cartilage, which is also known as articular cartilage. It's one of the key tissues in a healthy joint, acting as a shock absorber and providing a smooth surface between the bones. Cartilage consists of an arrangement of collagen fibres known as the matrix, which is filled with hyaluronic acid and chondroitin sulphate, among other components.

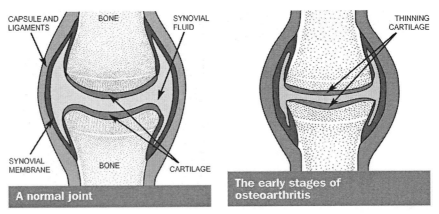

Courtesy of Arthritis Care

How osteoarthritis develops

Osteoarthritis develops when, with wear and tear, the cartilage starts to disintegrate, leaving the ends of the bones exposed. They then grind against each other, causing pain. The synovial membrane and joint capsule thicken, and space inside the joint narrows which leads to a stiff joint and pain.

Sometimes, part of the cartilage can break away from the bone leaving the bone ends exposed. These might then rub against each other and the ligaments become strained and weakened. This causes a lot of pain and changes the shape of the joint.

How it will affect you

The classic symptoms of osteoarthritis are swelling and stiffness in a joint, caused by the wearing away of the cartilage pads that protect and cushion the end of joints. This not only leads to inflammation, but can mean the bones grate against each other as they move. This can be extremely painful and moving your joint can be difficult.

Osteoarthritis is a condition that develops over time. Changes are usually slow and hard to detect in some people, whereas in others the pain and stiffness will gradually worsen until the disease process finishes.

At this point, the joints will look rather knobbly, but are often less painful, or even pain-free, and you should be able to carry out everyday tasks.

What causes osteoarthritis?

Although in many cases there is no specific cause, the risk of OA is greater if you have cartilage which doesn't repair itself 'normally', perhaps because of your genetic make-up. Nutrition and illness all have a role to play in developing the disease, as does how you take care of your joints and the muscles, ligaments and tendons around them. Injury to a joint can trigger osteoarthritis, even many years later.

Your bone structure is relevant too. If you are very bow-legged, your body weight passes more through the inner side of your knee and you are more at risk of developing osteoarthritis in that section.

Pressure over time

'In the same way as a car with a low annual mileage, driven in a sedate way, will last a long time, the same make and model of a car if thrashed, used for racing, or to carry heavy loads over a high mileage is likely to need replacing a lot sooner.'

The extent to which the body has been loaded over its lifetime will play some part. In the same way as a car with a low annual mileage, driven in a sedate way, will last a long time, the same make and model of a car if thrashed, used for racing, or to carry heavy loads over a high mileage is likely to need replacing a lot sooner. While some cars are better made than others, so some people seem to be better made than others, and some people look after themselves better than others.

If the surfaces of the joint are subjected to excessive loads over a prolonged period, they might start to wear out. This might happen in professional sports players, particularly if they have repeated minor injuries. It might also happen in people who are obese as their limbs have to carry more weight than the human body was designed for.

Case study

'I've had a problem with my left knee for a while (I'm 60 now) and occasionally it suddenly gives way without warning and if I walk too far it can be really painful. I think it's because I used to stand around a lot in my job and put a bit too much strain on my knee. I'm a bit bow-legged, so that probably doesn't help. I haven't been one to exercise that much either to be honest. My right knee isn't so bad – I'm not sure why. My doctor thinks I should consider a knee replacement but I'd rather wait and see how bad it gets. If I can still get out and play two or three rounds of golf a week, then I probably won't have the op, but if the pain and stiffness ever stopped me getting out on the golf course then I would consider having one.'

Robert from Norfolk

Shoulder problems

While shoulders have the greatest range of movement in the body the sockets are very shallow so the bones are more likely to slip out or dislocate.

The main risk for shoulder mobility is in fact not using the joint enough through its full range of movement. If the soft tissues around the joint contract and are not being stretched enough, the ball and socket get closer and the bones start to rub. The tissues and capsule around the joint become inflamed and the shoulder seizes up. This is known as capsulitus or 'frozen shoulder'.

A physiotherapist should be able to suggest exercises to free a frozen shoulder or you might be offered a procedure called 'manipulation under anaesthetic' to ease the problem.

How is osteoarthritis treated?

Treating osteoarthritis usually centres on relieving the pain and discomfort associated with the disease. Your doctor will prescribe you one (or more) of the following types of drugs:

Analgesics (painkillers).

Non-steroidal anti-inflammatory drugs (NSAIDs) which reduce inflammation and pain.

Steroids which also reduce inflammation in more severe cases of osteoarthritis and can be injected directly into a joint for fast relief.

You might be referred for further examinations such as an MRI scan or X-ray if your arthritis is severe or surgery is needed.

Early stages

In the early stages of osteoarthritis, it might be possible to alter the cause of the joint damage and allow healing to occur. For example, if the kneecap (patella) is not tracking properly over the front of the knee, it might wear away the cartilage on one side of the back of the patella, or front of the femur (thigh bone). Physiotherapy can help develop the muscle to correct the tracking.

Hyaluronic acid

There is some evidence to suggest hyaluronic acid might help relieve symptoms in early arthritis, and can be used for people who are keen to avoid surgery or for whom surgery would carry a high risk; for example if they are obese. The degree and length of benefit is a bit unpredictable, but it does seem relatively safe.

Importance of exercise

Exercise can help to maintain mobility, prevent stiffness and also strengthen the muscles that support the joints. It is the pumping mechanism that pushes nutrients into our joints, nourishing cartilage.

All living tissues respond to being loaded. If you lift weights, your muscles become stronger. Similarly, if you load them, your bones become stronger. This must also happen to cartilage, though it is harder to demonstrate. Regular exercise is therefore probably a good thing.

Cartilage isn't good at coping with high impact exercise and excessive load might cause repeated minor damage, which accounts for why so many professional sports players often develop arthritis in later life.

If your knees or hips are affected by osteoarthritis, then doing weight-bearing exercise can be difficult, but swimming is an excellent alternative, along with yoga and pilates. In many areas there are specialist classes for people with OA. (Your GP's surgery might have information on this). A physiotherapist could help with an exercise programme. Ask your GP if you could be referred on the NHS, otherwise you could go privately.

Top tips for keeping your joints moving

- Lose weight if you are overweight to reduce the strain on your weight-bearing joints.
- Stop smoking.
- Eat a healthy, well-balanced diet.

- Exercise regularly at a sensible level, avoiding injury, to strengthen your muscles – a physiotherapist can help with this.

- Massage painful joints and muscles.

- Try to relax – having a warm bath should help.

- Seek help early if you are starting to get problems.

- If you have a deformity, whether you were born with it, developed it as you grew up or as a result of an injury, consider having it corrected before it results in advanced arthritis.

Footwear

Wearing the right shoes is important to avoid damage to your ankles, knees and spine which could lead to osteoarthritis later on. Shoes with rubber soles absorb shocks better than leather ones. If you have flat feet, it's a good idea to wear insoles (a podiatrist can advise you on this) otherwise your feet might roll inwards, changing the position of the thigh bones. This in turn will lead to the pelvis tilting to accommodate the change, leading to misalignment and wearing.

Surgery – the options

Your doctor might refer you to an orthopaedic surgeon if you have severe arthritis affecting weight-bearing joints, such as the knees.

Surgery can be a smaller procedure, such as a 'debridement' which is tidying up the joint, possibly reshaping the bone; or more major procedures such as an osteotomy, which involves cutting the bone near the joint to change the angle; often used for the knee.

Other surgery includes fusion (joining the two bones together, usually in smaller joints such as the wrist, toes and ankle) and replacement with an artificial joint.

'Wearing the right shoes is important to avoid damage to your ankles, knees and spine which could lead to osteoarthritis later on.'

Knee replacements

The knee is the most complicated joint in the body, and 5-10 times our body weight goes through the joint with every step. A common operation on the knee is an arthroscopy to remove torn cartilage and restore normal function to the joint.

Whether or not you have the operation will depend on the level of pain you are experiencing and if the joint is unstable. Only you know how much pain is bearable for you and how much the problem is affecting your daily life. You can discuss the pros and cons of having the operation with your surgeon. Surgery is avoided if at all possible, as it does carry some risks.

Partial replacements

Around 80,000 people have knee replacements each year in England and Wales. If only part of the knee is damaged, replacing only that part might be considered by a surgeon. Generally speaking, a surgeon would try to perform the smallest operation, doing the least damage, to resolve the problem.

This does mean that if the other parts wear out in the future, they might need replacing eventually and most surgeons would do this by removing the partial knee replacement and inserting a total knee replacement.

Figures from the UK National Joint Register show there is a higher rate of further surgery in partial knee replacements compared to total knee replacements. This might have something to do with sufferers coming back with arthritis in the part of the knee that wasn't replaced.

As a rule, it seems better to avoid a total knee replacement for as long as possible, although it can work well for ten years or even longer for many people.

Other operations

If you're bow-legged and starting to develop pain on the inner side of the knee, by straightening out the limb with a corrective operation on the bone, it might be possible to move the limb into a normal alignment before the joint is too badly damaged. Similar, though more complex, operations can be performed around the hip and in other places too.

Summing Up

As we live longer, various bits of our bodies will continue to wear out. However, by avoiding injury and taking proper exercise, we can all do our bit to help protect our joints and avoid surgery, or the need for an artificial joint replacement in the future.

The key is to seek help as soon as you start to experience problems and not wait until your osteoarthritis is severe. Early intervention offers the best chance to limit any damage to your joints - and keep you on the move.

With special thanks to orthopaedic surgeon Stephen Krikler of the British Orthopaedic Association (www.boa.ac.uk) for his help in compiling this chapter. Arthritis Care has produced a booklet with further information on living with osteoarthritis and ways to look after your joints, which can be downloaded from their website www.arthritiscare.org.uk.

Chapter Two

Rheumatoid Arthritis (RA)

Rheumatoid arthritis, or RA as it is also known, is the second most common form of arthritis after osteoarthritis. An estimated 700,000 people have RA in the UK alone.

Although RA is a progressive, long-term condition, existing treatments are generally effective in relieving symptoms and controlling disease progression; and with earlier diagnosis and improved standards of care, people with RA can live a relatively normal life.

What is rheumatoid arthritis?

Rheumatoid arthritis is an inflammatory autoimmune disease that mainly affects joints and tendons. It often begins in the wrists, hands or feet and can spread to other joints, making them stiffen and swell and feel warm to the touch.

RA can start gradually or suddenly, when for no known reason, the body's immune system starts attacking and damaging joints and soft tissues surrounding the bones. The disease generally affects both sides of the body – not always at once, but usually soon after symptoms first appear. It can also make you feel as if you have flu, and fatigue is often an issue for people.

Who is likely to develop RA?

Although it can start at any age, you are more likely to develop RA between 30 and 55. It affects many more women than men, and babies, children and adolescents can also get a form of it - juvenile idiopathic arthritis (JIA). There are approximately 12,000 children under 16 with JIA in the UK.

'With earlier diagnosis and improved standards of care, people with rheumatoid arthritis can live a relatively normal life.'

Everyone's disease is different

Although RA can be a painful condition, sometimes causing disability, its intensity can vary considerably between people. But ultimately, without effective treatment, the result is the same: some damage to cartilage and bone around the joints.

As RA is a systemic disease, it can affect the whole body and sometimes organs such as lungs, heart and eyes are involved.

Early treatment

If RA is not controlled, there is an increased risk of cardiovascular disease, such as heart attacks and strokes. Added to which, most of the damage to joints can happen in the first months and years of RA, so it is vital to get the disease diagnosed and treated as quickly as possible.

Inflammation – the effects

Inflammation is usually the body's way of healing, but with RA the immune system starts to attack the body cells instead of defending them.

This inflammation can damage tissues that line the joint capsule and lubricate the muscle tendons to allow them to move smoothly over each other. The cartilage and bone are also damaged, and ultimately the whole joint might be weakened and deformed.

Case study

'My arthritis began in 1994 with a stiff neck and a fairly mild pain in the balls of my feet. The pain gradually worsened so I made an appointment with my GP. I was probably a complete stranger to him because of my good health. As soon as I described my symptoms he explained that it sounded like rheumatoid arthritis.

'To say that I was in shock was an understatement. My future was flashing in front of my eyes. I feared that I would lose my job and that my wife and children would be homeless because I would not be able to pay the mortgage.

'I kept all my concerns to myself and did not tell my wife about what was going on in my head. I felt that there was no point in us both panicking. I did not understand how I could be so healthy and get such a debilitating disease. I ate well, cycled over 600 miles per month and worked full-time as a factory manager.

'Later on, I discovered that rheumatoid arthritis ran in our family. I knew nothing then of self-help groups or where to turn for help and information and the Internet was still in its infancy.

'I tried a whole range of medication in the 10 years that followed. Then it occurred to me that I could take more control of my arthritis through changes to my lifestyle. I began exercising for 30 minutes every morning and kept a log of my diet, weight and exercise. I replaced junk food with fish and fruit and vegetables, and drank green tea instead of beer (most of the time, anyway). I felt that I had to be in the best possible condition to win this battle.

'It is great to have reduced my medication and feel I have beaten my arthritis. It is just like a bad memory and, for now, I can enjoy swinging from the trees with my grandchildren.'

Dennis from Northern Ireland. Courtesy of Arthritis Care www.arthritiscare.org.uk

What causes RA?

Nature and nurture

No one really knows what causes Rheumatoid Arthritis. Certain genes which play a part in the immune system are linked to RA, but having these genes doesn't mean you will definitely develop RA; but you will have a tendency towards it. Genes might also determine the response you might have to treatment with a specific drug.

However, some people with the genes will never get RA and others who have RA don't always have the genes. Researchers now think that an environmental trigger occurs which causes RA in people who have a genetic tendency to develop it. These triggers include:

'Flare-ups can be over in a couple of days or last for a month or so.'

- Stress.
- Smoking.
- An injury or trauma.
- An infection or virus.
- Hormonal changes, such as pregnancy or the menopause, which can cause the immune system to malfunction.

What are the symptoms?

The symptoms of RA vary, sometimes from day to day, but are usually defined by stiffness, particularly when you get up in the morning, swelling, pain and fatigue. There might be times when the disease is active (a flare-up) and the symptoms are worse. Flare-ups can be over in a couple of days or last for a month or so. At other times when the disease is inactive you might feel much better. Fatigue is something which many people find almost as challenging as the pain and this is a very common symptom.

How to cope during a flare-up

Increasing your painkillers or anti-inflammatory drugs, with your doctor's approval, might help. Resting the joint in neutral position – perhaps with a splint – will help minimise any damage; and gently keeping the rest of your joints moving will stop them getting stiff. Warm water and heat can also help, as can ice packs (or frozen peas wrapped in a tea towel) for inflamed joints.

Take the time out to do something you enjoy, to distract you. And remember, while flare-ups can be demanding, they will pass. Although steroids (see page 26) are no longer seen as the mainstay of therapy, an injection of steroid into the joint(s) affected, or into the buttock, might provide rapid relief.

Diagnosis

There's no single test for rheumatoid arthritis, and diagnosis can be complicated. Your doctor will ask you about the difficulties you've been experiencing; as well as examine your joints and skin, and test your muscle strength.

You should then be referred to a rheumatologist for tests, such as blood tests or X-rays, if some form of inflammatory arthritis is suspected. These tests will help the doctor get a better picture of what is going on and show if there is a high level of inflammation present. These tests are likely to include erythrocyte sedimentation rate (ESR) and C-reactive protein (CRP).

Some people with RA have raised inflammation levels, while others don't. Acute disease and severe disease cause raised levels. Normal levels might indicate remission.

You should also be tested to see if you have the rheumatoid factor, RF, or a more modern equivalent (CCP), although these are not always present, particularly in the early stages of the disease. Some people who go on to develop RA do not have rheumatoid factor – this is known as seronegative disease.

Other tests might include an assessment of bone density (DXA) as thin bones (osteoporosis) are common in RA.

How is RA treated?

Your doctor will take into account a number of factors when deciding on the right treatment for you, such as the severity of your symptoms and how the condition affects your body and your everyday life.

Your DAS, or disease activity score, should be taken as well. This is a composite score comprising of a measurement for swelling and tenderness in 28 of your joints. It is an estimate by you of how severely your disease is affecting you on a scale of 1-10 (where 10 is the worst) - coupled with the results of a blood test where your ESR and CRP are measured.

The National Rheumatoid Arthritis Society (NRAS) produces a booklet to help you understand what DAS is and how it can help in the treatment of your condition. There is also a DVD on their website which you can watch (www.nras.org.uk).

Treatment options

There are different types of drug treatments, taken on their own or in combination, for rheumatoid arthritis. Some tackle pain; others inflammation, and some are used to try to slow the course of the disease (DMARDs).

It is not unusual to try out several therapies before finding something that suits you, and over time your treatment might need to be adjusted. Treatments include:

Painkillers (analgesics) and NSAIDs (anti-inflammatory drugs)

Most people with rheumatoid arthritis need some form of pain relief. As painkillers don't tackle the underlying reason for the pain, they are usually prescribed in combination with drugs that do. The anti-inflammatories such as ibuprofen, diclofenac and naprosyn are more effective than simple analgesics but can cause tummy trouble. The COX 2 inhibitors such as celecoxib, are a newer type of NSAID, designed to be safer for the stomach.

DMARDs

These are disease-modifying anti-rheumatoid drugs, or immunosuppressives, that dampen down the effects of the immune system's attack on the joints. Most are taken orally (by mouth) and occasionally by injection which usually has fewer side effects. The 'gold standard' is methotrexate, which is usually taken with a folic acid supplement. Methotrexate can be taken orally or by sub-cutaneous (under the skin) injection.

Other DMARDs include sulphasalazine, leflunomide and an anti-malarial such as hydroxychloroquine sulphate.

Biologics

In the last 10 years or so, a group of drugs called Biologics have revolutionised the treatment of RA. This group of drugs includes anti-TNFs which block the action of a chemical called tumour necrosis factor (TNF). TNF plays an important role in driving the inflammation and tissue damage of rheumatoid arthritis, and anti-TNFs might be able to delay or even prevent this.

You might be prescribed etanercept (Enbrel), adalimumab (Humira) or certolizumab (Cimzia), given by injection, or infliximab, given by infusion every 8 weeks in hospital. There is a fifth anti-TNF, which is not yet widely available, called golimumab (Simponi), also given by injection. There are also other biologic therapies, which you might be prescribed, which target different chemicals to anti-TNF.

Though anti-TNFs do not work for everyone, and might not be suitable for all, they can offer good control to some people with severe rheumatoid arthritis who have not responded well to other disease-modifying drugs. They are usually taken in conjunction with methotrexate or another DMARD. (The NRAS website has a booklet *Biologics, The Story so Far*, which explains more).

'In the last 10 years or so, a group of drugs called Biologics have revolutionised the treatment of rheumatoid arthritis.'

Steroids

Corticosteroids (steroids), such as prednisolone, given by injection or taken as a tablet, can be very effective in reducing inflammation. Your doctor will try to give you the lowest effective dose and you will be carefully monitored. (You should not alter the dose yourself, or stop taking steroids suddenly).

Steroids are generally used as 'bridging' medication to help newly-diagnosed patients while waiting for their DMARDs to start working, or, as mentioned earlier, for treatment during a flare-up. Current evidence-based guidelines advise against giving steroids longterm.

Surgery

Although you won't necessarily need any operations for your RA, surgery is another way of relieving pain, keeping your joints working and preventing disability - but has to be considered carefully.

Joint replacement surgery is usually only discussed if the joint is very painful or if there is a risk you might lose overall function. It is important, however, to seek early surgical advice if you are experiencing extreme pain in a joint, rather than soldiering on and allowing the joint to become very damaged.

Progress of the disease

As rheumatoid arthritis progresses, it can start to destroy the cartilage and bone within the joint and weaken the surrounding muscles and tissues. When this happens, the joint becomes unstable. This is when surgery can be very helpful.

For some people, RA can be mild, resulting in only minor damage to their joints. Others will have very active arthritis for many years, and a series of bad flare-ups. Several joints can be involved and rheumatoid arthritis is likely to have a serious impact on their lives.

About 10% of RA sufferers can come off their treatment without recurrence and these people might have a self-limiting form of RA. This is more likely where the RF and CCP are negative.

Managing your arthritis

The part you play is vital. Only you know how you feel and the sort of help you need most. You have to take charge of your arthritis and learn how to manage it – which will become easier over time.

It is important to take extra care of your joints as soon as you are diagnosed. Spread the load by using both hands to lift objects, and protect the fragile joints in your fingers and wrists by using your shoulder or hip instead where possible. And watch your posture - slouching can put extra pressure on muscles and joints.

Your doctor can refer you to an occupational therapist who will advise you on how to make the most efficient use of your joints without causing further damage.

A physiotherapist can prepare exercises to keep your muscles strong and retain a good range of movement in your joints. People with RA are treated by a consultant-led multidisciplinary team which should include access to a specialist nurse, occupational therapist, occupational health advisor (for workplace assessments and help with employment issues), physiotherapists and podiatrists.

'The part you play is vital. Only you know how you feel and the sort of help you need most.'

Top tips for managing RA

There are other things you can do to help manage your condition including:

▓ Rest your joints when your arthritis flares up badly - but don't rest them for too long as they could stiffen.

▓ Ask for help and support from others if you need it.

▓ Adjust your lifestyle – don't take on too much.

▓ If your symptoms worsen, or you think the treatment isn't working, tell your rheumatologist.

▓ Keep mobile and exercise regularly – swimming and yoga can help.

▓ Eat a healthy diet with plenty of fruit and vegetables.

▓ Don't smoke.

▓ Lose excess weight to relieve pressure on your joints.

▓ Keep going – even if it feels as though nothing is working.

Summing Up

Coping with RA is not easy for anyone, but remember you are not alone. Work with your medical team to get the right treatment to relieve your symptoms, and discover new skills to help you adapt. While there is no cure for the disease, and for most people RA is a condition for life, the good news is that the prospects of a better quality of life are so much better now with new treatments such as Biologics, to help control the disease. And remember, your RA is only part of your life – not the whole of it.

With special thanks to the National Rheumatoid Arthritis Society (NRAS) www.nras.org.uk and the British Society of Rheumatology www.rheumatology.org.uk for their assistance in compiling this chapter.

Chapter Three

Seronegative Arthritis: Ankylosing Spondylitis (AS)

Seronegative arthritis is a general term describing the kinds of inflammatory arthritis where a specific antibody, known as rheumatoid factor, or RF, doesn't show up in blood tests.

The early stages of rheumatoid arthritis can also be called seronegative arthritis as the test for RF is less likely to be positive in the first few months after symptoms start.

Seronegative RA tends to be a less severe form of inflammatory arthritis with a different set of symptoms, although usually it's treated in the same way as rheumatoid arthritis.

Types of seronegative arthritis

The main forms of seronegative arthritis are:

Psoriatic arthritis

Psoriatic arthritis is an inflammatory joint disease which usually affects people who already have psoriasis - a skin complaint that causes a red, scaly rash, especially on the elbows, knees, back and scalp. However, some people develop the arthritis symptoms first, and some never develop the skin disease.

As with most arthritic conditions, the symptoms are stiffness, pain and lack of movement in affected areas, particularly the joints in the hands and feet. Knees, elbows and hips can also be swollen and painful.

Reactive arthritis

As the name suggests, reactive arthritis can develop as the result of a reaction in the body to a virus, stomach infection, food poisoning, a sexually transmitted infection (STI) or a life-changing event. Some people have been known to develop reactive arthritis after swimming in the Nile in Egypt.

Reactive arthritis is fairly rare, with only around 40 new cases diagnosed each year. Reactive arthritis connected to an STI is more common in men than women, while men and women equally can develop reactive arthritis after a stomach infection or food poisoning.

Ankylosing Spondylitis

We will be concentrating on ankylosing spondylitis in this chapter.

What is ankylosing spondylitis?

'Ankylosing spondylitis, or AS for short, is a progressive form of arthritis which mainly affects the spine. An estimated 200,000 people in the UK have AS.'

Ankylosing spondylitis, or AS for short, is a progressive form of arthritis which mainly affects the spine, although other joints, tendons and ligaments can be involved. An estimated 200,000 people in the UK have AS.

With AS, some or all of the joints and bones of the spine bind together. The name comes from the Greek words for fusing (ankylosing) and inflammation of the vertebrae, or backbone (spondylitis).

Entire fusing of the spine is rare and most people with AS will have only a partial fusion that is sometimes limited to the pelvic bones. The pelvis is commonly affected first. The lower back, chest wall and neck might also become involved at different times.

The fusing process

Inflammation occurs at the site where certain ligaments or tendons attach to the bone. The inflammation is followed by some erosion (wearing away) of the bone at the site of the attachment.

As the inflammation subsides, a healing process takes place and new bone develops. As a result, movement becomes restricted where bone replaces the elastic tissue of ligaments or tendons.

When inflammation occurs again, more bone is formed and the individual bones which make up your vertebrae bind together, causing the pain and stiffness of AS.

Common symptoms of AS

Some people with AS have no obvious symptoms, whereas others might have severe ones. The common symptoms, which usually last for more than three months, include:

- Slow or gradual onset of back pain and stiffness over weeks or months, not days.
- Early morning stiffness and pain which wears-off or reduces during the day with exercise.
- Feeling better after exercise and worse after rest.
- Weight loss – especially early on in the disease.
- Fatigue.
- Feeling feverish with night sweats.

Who is likely to develop AS?

Anyone, including children, can develop AS, although usually they are affected in slightly different ways.

Women

The pelvis, hips, knees, wrists and ankles are mainly involved.

Men

The pelvis and spine are affected (known as axial disease) although other joints might be involved, including the chest wall, hips, shoulders and feet (known as peripheral disease).

Children

Children under the age of 11 rarely develop symptoms of AS. If they do, the knees, ankles and feet are usually affected.

What causes AS?

While the definite cause is not known, it is thought people who have a genetic predisposition to AS might come into contact with some normally harmless micro-organism, setting off an adverse reaction. Sometimes bowel infections can trigger AS.

AS and other arthritic conditions

People with AS can have other arthritic conditions at the same time, including osteoarthritis, which is caused by wear and tear on the joints over time.

Case study

'I developed AS when I was around 18. I was very athletic, played county tennis for Surrey and Sussex, and Junior Wimbledon. I had tennis elbow a lot, and later pain and stiffness in my hips and back. Then, very gradually, my joints started to seize up - my back first, then my hips and then my neck. It was a slow process. I've heard AS does burn itself out as time goes on, and I think that's happened with me. I don't see a rheumatologist anymore, as my GP seems able to deal with it. I don't think it does affect me in a big way. It's a bit like driving a car with bad brakes: you adjust your driving to accommodate them. It does restrict my movement though - especially bending down to pick things up and putting on my socks, etc but I can still do most things. I walk a lot and play tennis quite happily but anything with any impact, like running, I find painful.

'I'd encourage anyone with AS to exercise a lot so you stay mobile; keep medication to a minimum, and eat well. I find the sun and heat help me a lot too. The cold and damp make it worse and bring on aches and pains, so I try to head to the sun as much as possible!'

Mathew from Suffolk

'I'd encourage anyone with AS to exercise a lot so you stay mobile; keep medication to a minimum, and eat well.'

Mathew from Suffolk.

How is AS diagnosed?

It is important to get an early diagnosis of AS to prevent any long-term damage to joints and tissues.

If you think you might have AS, particularly if you have inflammatory back pain, see your GP as soon as possible. Let him or her know what your symptoms are; how long you have had them; how they started – suddenly or slowly over time – and the impact your symptoms are having on your home and working life.

If your doctor thinks you might have AS you will be referred to a rheumatologist to confirm the diagnosis. Blood tests will usually be taken to help make a firm diagnosis of AS, and rule out any other inflammatory arthritic condition like rheumatoid arthritis.

Genetic test

You will probably be tested for the HLA-B27 gene as approximately 95% of people with AS carry this particular gene. However, only around 8% of people who carry the HLA-B27 gene will go on to develop AS; so this gene alone is not responsible for triggering AS.

A number of other genes might be involved in making people prone to AS. Work underway by researchers in the Genetic Research Programme could help pinpoint what these genes are - and hopefully increase understanding of AS.

Further tests

These might include X-rays and MRI scans as well as an assessment of your joint flexibility and any tenderness you might be experiencing.

How is AS treated?

Once you have a firm diagnosis, your rheumatologist will discuss a course of treatment with you, to relieve pain and stiffness; to help reduce the inflammation and to lessen the impact of the disease on your joints and tissues. Your rheumatologist should refer you for physiotherapy as part of your treatment programme.

Depending on the severity of your AS, your doctor might need to give you a combination of medications, or just one. The groups of medicines used to treat AS include:

Painkillers (analgesics)

These reduce pain and are often used together with other medications for AS. They should also help you carry on exercising – vital for managing AS.

Non-steroidal anti-inflammatory drugs (NSAIDs)

These reduce inflammation as well as pain. Ibuprofen and diclofenac are types of NSAIDs in common use.

Steroids (corticosteroids)

These drugs are very effective in controlling inflammation. They can be used in the form of local injections into joints, or in tablet form taken orally.

Disease-modifying ant-rheumatoid drugs (DMARDs)

This group of drugs, which includes methotrexate, is used less commonly in AS, but can reduce pain, stiffness and swelling in people who have symptoms of AS in areas such as the hips, knees, ankles or wrists, rather than in the spine.

Anti-TNF therapy

This can only be prescribed by rheumatologists to people with severe AS. Currently adalimumab (Humira) and etanercept (Enbrel) are the forms available to people with AS.

'Aside from taking appropriate medication, there is so much you can do to help manage your AS.'

Top tips for managing AS

Aside from taking appropriate medication, there is so much you can do to help manage your AS, reduce your symptoms and improve the outcome of your condition. These include:

- Tell your doctor if your medication isn't working or your symptoms change.
- Stop smoking.
- Lose excess weight to reduce pressure on your joints.
- Eat a healthy, balanced diet with lots of fruit and vegetables.
- Try to be positive and enjoy life.

Importance of exercise

Appropriate exercise is important in the management of AS and can have a real impact on the prognosis of the condition, helping to maintain flexibility and avoid fusion. A physiotherapist can advise you on the right exercise programme for you. Ask your doctor if you can be referred on the NHS, or you might have to consult a physiotherapist privately.

Spondylosis

While AS is a form of inflammatory arthritis, spondylosis is a medical term for the general wear and tear that occurs in the joints and bones of the spine as we get older. Cervical spondylosis specifically refers to wear and tear in the section of spine in the neck (the cervical spine). It causes periods of stiffness and pain in the neck that could spread to the shoulders, and the base of the skull.

Spondylosis is an age-related condition and it is estimated that almost everyone will have some symptoms of cervical spondylosis by the age of 70. This means that people with AS might also start to develop symptoms of spondylosis as they get older.

Summing Up

AS is a long-term inflammatory condition which affects the lives of those with the illness to varying degrees. It is estimated that around a third of people with AS are not able to work because of their problems, and where people do suffer curvature of the spine or neck, it can severely impact on their quality of life.

Yet with the use of effective treatments, improved standards of care and regular, appropriate exercise, the disease can be managed effectively, allowing most AS sufferers to lead relatively normal lives.

With special thanks to the National Ankylosing Spondylitis Society (NASS) for their help in compiling this chapter. www.nass.co.uk

Chapter Four

Lupus (SLE)

Chances are a lot of people have never have heard of lupus, or have no clear idea what the condition entails. Yet lupus is more common than leukaemia and multiple sclerosis, with an estimated 5 million sufferers worldwide. Around 50,000 people in the UK live with lupus.

The term lupus comes from the Latin word for wolf and refers to lupus vulgaris, wolf's bite - a severe facial rash which affected people with lupus, although it isn't seen that often now.

What is lupus?

Lupus, or to give it its full name, systemic lupus erythematosus, or SLE, is an autoimmune disease which sends someone's immune system into overdrive, attacking the body's own tissues. As a result, too many antibodies are produced, causing inflammation almost anywhere in the body. More serious complications of lupus can involve the kidneys, brain and blood. Lupus is neither infectious nor contagious.

There are two types of lupus: SLE and discoid. Discoid lupus is a condition of the skin alone, but in a few patients can develop into systemic lupus. This chapter will concentrate on systemic lupus.

Who is likely to develop lupus?

People of Afro-Caribbean, Asian and Far Eastern origin are more likely to develop lupus, although women from anywhere in the world can get the disease. It usually attacks women of child-bearing age.

Men can suffer too, although in far fewer numbers. The ratio of female to male sufferers is 9:1. Often symptoms are more severe in men than in women.

'Around 50,000 people in the UK live with lupus.'

What causes lupus?

No one really knows, although genetics do play a part. Quite often people with lupus have family members with this condition, or other autoimmune diseases such as multiple sclerosis. Lupus sufferers sometimes have a history of allergies - frequently developing skin rashes, for example - and are more likely to suffer side effects to various drugs than people without the disease.

Triggers

There are a number of possible triggers in those with a predisposition to lupus including:

- Rashes (sometimes sun-sensitive).
- A viral infection.
- Strong medication.
- Trauma.
- Hormonal changes such as puberty, pregnancy and the menopause.
- Environmental factors.

What are the symptoms of lupus?

Symptoms vary depending on the severity of the condition but usually include:

- Extreme fatigue.
- Anaemia.
- Eye problems.
- Mouth or nasal ulcers.
- Miscarriage – sometimes recurrent.
- Joint or muscle pain.
- Depression.

- Facial or other rashes.
- Hair loss.
- Fever.
- Possible involvement of the kidneys, heart, lungs and brain.

How is lupus diagnosed?

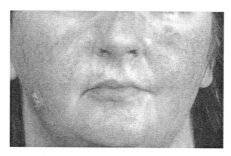

Courtesy of St Thomas' Lupus Trust

Diagnosis isn't easy as lupus has a range of symptoms which could be mistaken by GPs, not familiar with the condition, as other diseases such as multiple sclerosis, leukaemia or muscular dystrophy.

Your GP will take into account your full medical history and if any family members have the condition, and arrange blood tests.

Blood tests

These are likely to include ESR and CRP, which measure the levels of inflammation in your body, and an anti-DNA test which shows if there are any lupus antibodies in your system. A positive anti-DNA test doesn't prove someone has lupus, and a negative one doesn't prove they haven't. But along with typical symptoms, these tests can help a doctor make a diagnosis.

If a lupus diagnosis is suspected, your doctor will then refer you to a rheumatologist for further examination and to confirm the diagnosis.

'Diagnosis isn't easy as lupus has a range of symptoms which could be mistaken by GPs, not familiar with the condition, as other diseases such as multiple sclerosis, leukaemia or muscular dystrophy.'

Further examination

Your rheumatologist will check whether four out of eleven accepted conditions that they use to diagnose lupus - such as someone having a skin rash and muscle and joint pain – are met. They will then prescribe a suitable course of treatment as soon as possible to relieve the symptoms and get the condition under control.

Other specialists

As lupus can affect any organ of the body, other specialists, including dermatologists (skin experts) might be involved to confirm a lupus diagnosis.

How is lupus treated?

When you're diagnosed, you'll be carefully monitored and your symptoms kept under control as much as possible with suitable treatments.

People with mild symptoms might not need any medication. For those with more severe symptoms the following treatments might be used:

Non-steroidals (NSAIDs)

These are used for people whose symptoms are mainly joint or muscle pain. There are over 40 different non-steroidals available, such as brufen, motrin, orudis, naprosyn, feldene, fenoprofen and voltarol. They usually achieve the same results, although some patients find one type of non-steroidal works for them better than another.

Anti-malarials

Anti-malarials often provide sufficient treatment for patients with moderately active lupus. The three most widely used drugs in this category are chloroquine phosphate (Nivaquine), mepacrine (Quinacrine Atabrin) and hydroxychloroquine (Plaquenil).

Anti-malarials stopped being prescribed by doctors for a while because of side effects, such as impaired vision, if taken in high doses. But with the smaller doses now used (and with annual eye checks) the risk of damage to the eyes is believed to be very small.

Steroids

Treatment with steroids, or corticosteroids to give them their full name, has proved effective in treating lupus. The most commonly used steroid is prednisolone. When steroids came on the scene in the 1950s, lupus was one of the first conditions in which they were used - with impressive results.

However with the current knowledge of the long-term as well as the short-term side effects of steroids, such as thinning skin and osteoporosis, they're used less often now to treat lupus.

DMARDs

If other treatments aren't working, your rheumatologist might prescribe disease-modifying drugs (DMARDs), which tackle the underlying causes.

These include methotrexate, and more recently mycophenolate mofetil or MMF which has been used in transplants. Of course these have side effects too and your treatment will be carefully monitored using blood tests.

New treatments

Many of the drugs currently prescribed for lupus are effective, but their use has been based in the past on clinical experience and small studies.

Over the past few years the big pharmaceutical companies have taken a great interest in SLE and have financed a number of major trials, but none of these trials has shown any major benefits over existing treatments – until now. A positive study carried out by Human Genome Sciences using a drug called belimumab (trade name Benlysta) is showing promising results.

'When steroids came on the scene in the 1950s, lupus was one of the first conditions in which they were used – with impressive results.'

This drug works by reducing the ability of b-cells in the immune system to produce lupus antibodies. Antibodies produced by b-cells include anti-DNA antibodies which are associated with active lupus, especially kidney disease.

In the largest ever clinical trial including 865 patients in 90 clinics around the world, belimumab showed a significantly better treatment response compared to patients who had been given placebos (fake pills).

It's hoped after a further study the drug could be licensed as a lupus treatment within two years. Although it is not a cure for lupus, the new drug is considered by doctors to be a major advance in the treatment of patients with moderately severe lupus who have not responded to standard treatments.

Is lupus for life?

Lupus is a long-term condition with no cure, but with the right treatment and a positive attitude most people with lupus can lead a near-normal life.

It's possible for lupus sufferers to have their condition under control as doctors are tailoring medication to an individual's needs, and the future for lupus sufferers is much brighter than a decade ago.

There's increasing evidence that many people with lupus are not so reliant on their medication, and visits to their doctor or rheumatologist are less frequent, if they help manage their illness.

Top tips for managing lupus

Your role in the management of your condition is very important. Only you know how you feel and whether you can manage on a daily basis. So it's important to consider the following:

■ Watch your symptoms and let your consultant and GP know if they change or you have a reaction to your medication.

■ Learn to pace yourself and don't take on too much.

■ Make sure family and friends are aware of the unpredictable nature of the condition and the depression and pain that can accompany it.

- Eat a healthy diet. Some people with lupus find low-GI foods which release energy slowly – such as wholemeal bread, brown rice and steamed vegetables - help.

- Include regular gentle exercise into your daily routine to keep you mobile, but don't overdo it

- Take advice before going in the sun.

- Don't smoke.

- Stay positive – it will help you control your symptoms, and people who stay upbeat usually cope better.

Louise Coote Specialist Lupus Unit

In most hospitals, lupus is part of the general rheumatology service. But at St Thomas' in London, there's a highly specialist unit within the NHS for anyone with lupus. The Louise Coote Unit, named after a patient with lupus who was treated at the hospital, is the largest lupus unit in Europe. Patients can be referred by their GP to the unit from anywhere in the UK.

'Lupus is a weird illness in the fact that it makes you tired but then won't let you sleep. Many patients find great difficulty in sleeping more than a few hours a night and the sleep quality is very poor.'

Angie, Campaign Director of St Thomas' Lupus Trust

Case study

'Lupus is a weird illness in the fact that it makes you tired but then won't let you sleep. Many patients find great difficulty in sleeping more than a few hours a night and the sleep quality is very poor, often tossing and turning most of the night. By July of 2005 I had gone from about 4-5 hours sleep a night to, on some nights, literally one! This obviously couldn't continue so I asked Dr David D'Cruz if there was anything I could do to help me sleep (apart from sleeping tablets which I wanted only as a very last resort).

'He told me that they had just completed trials with lupus patients following the low glycaemic index diet (low GI) and most patients reported much less fatigue. This obviously sounded worth trying, especially as I was getting quite desperate at this stage.

'I started the diet on 14th July and within 3 months had lost 2 stone (which my knees thanked me for!). I was much, much less tired and was happily getting 8 hours undisturbed sleep a night. My joint pains were less and people that hadn't seen me for a while described me as 'glowing'. I had to admit I'd never felt better. I am still following the principles of the diet and still sleep well and feel great. (For more details of the research go to www.lupus.org.uk).

I look forward to the end of the menopause as often women report that lupus goes into remission then as it's not being triggered by hormonal surges. In December 2009 I was pleased to say that I ran 5k for the charity and was actually more impressed that I did it at my age than with lupus! Shows what you can do if you put your mind to it, and prepare for it.'

Angie, Campaign Director of St Thomas' Lupus Trust.

Summing Up

Although lupus is a chronic disease that can be debilitating, with proper care and the right treatment the condition can be managed effectively, allowing you to lead a near-normal life within a near-normal lifespan. And the earlier you get a proper diagnosis the better the outcome is likely to be.

So if you suspect you might have the disease – perhaps a family member has had it or you develop a rash and muscle and joint pain – go to your GP as soon as possible and ask for a referral to a rheumatologist for a definite diagnosis. The quicker you see a specialist, the earlier your treatment can begin and your disease put under control.

With treatments improving, and more awareness of the disease among the medical profession, a diagnosis of lupus today is not as frightening as it would have been even ten years ago, and the outlook is considerably brighter.

With special thanks to St Thomas' Lupus Trust (www.lupus.org.uk) for their assistance in compiling this chapter.

Chapter Five

Polymyalgia Rheumatica (PMR)

Polymyalgia rheumatica, or PMR, is an autoimmune condition that involves many (poly) painful muscles (myalgia). The condition is characterised by tenderness, pain and stiffness in soft tissues, usually around the shoulders, hips, upper arms and thighs.

PMR is occasionally associated with giant cell arteritis (GCA, sometimes called temporal arteritis) which is inflammation of the temporal arteries, with 'giant cells' seen under the microscope. If not diagnosed and treated quickly, GCA can lead to sudden blindness.

'Polymyalgia rheumatica, or PMR, is an autoimmune condition that involves many (poly) painful muscles (myalgia).'

Who is likely to develop PMR?

PMR is the most frequently occurring inflammatory rheumatological condition among people over 65 in the UK; with one in 100 people over this age developing it. The average age of onset is 70, and PMR rarely affects anyone under 60.

Older women are twice as likely to get PMR as older men. It is also much more common in people of white, European and Scandinavian origin.

How is PMR diagnosed?

PMR can be difficult to diagnose as it can be confused with general aches and pains, osteoarthritis or an infection. There is no blood test for PMR, although research is underway to develop one. A raised ESR, or other blood test for inflammation, can indicate inflammation is present, but you can have PMR or GCA without having a raised ESR – although this is rare.

What causes PMR?

Little is known about the causes. PMR is thought to be partly genetic. Sometimes the condition can develop after a traumatic or stressful event, or an infection, such as flu.

What are the symptoms?

PMR usually comes on suddenly, or appears over a week or two, sometimes just after a flu-like illness. You might go to bed feeling fine, but wakeup feeling stiff. Early morning stiffness, which eases as the day progresses, is one of the most significant symptoms. PMR tends to come and go and sufferers can go into remission or become free of symptoms. Other common symptoms include:

■ Finding it hard to turn over in bed, get out of bed or dress yourself.

■ Pain in your neck or shoulder muscles which lessens when you move.

■ Stiffness after sitting for any length of time.

How is PMR treated?

The pain of PMR can be greatly reduced by taking glucocorticoids, also called corticosteroids or often just steroids. Steroids reduce inflammation in our bodies. The most common type of steroid given by doctors for PMR is called prednisolone. It is taken as a tablet, or by injection.

In most cases of PMR, doctors would prescribe a medium dose to start with – usually 15mg daily - and then gradually reduce it until you are taking the lowest dose (a maintenance dose) to control the PMR. It might take a while to get the dose right.

As steroids can have side effects, it is important to take the exact dose prescribed by your doctor.

Never stop taking steroids suddenly, as this can be dangerous. You should be given a steroid card to carry so that if you see another doctor, or have an accident, people are aware you are taking steroids.

How long will the treatment last?

Treatment usually lasts around two years, but this is not always the case.

The majority of sufferers have no further symptoms of their PMR once they get onto the correct treatment. A significant minority (perhaps a third) will have a relapse and have to increase their treatment for a while; a few of them will find they have to continue with a small dose of steroid indefinitely.

Possible side effects of steroids

Steroids can control the stiffness and sometimes the pain of PMR within a few days. Taking steroids also protects you from the eye problems which can occur with GCA.

The longer you take steroids for or the higher the dose, the more likely you are to get side effects. The most common ones are:

- Putting on weight.
- A round 'moon' face.
- Easy bruising.
- Stretch marks.
- Thinning of the skin.
- Cataracts in the eyes.
- A rise in your blood sugar level. If you have diabetes, you might need to change your medication.
- A rise in your blood pressure (on high doses of steroids)
- Susceptibility to infections.

Always tell your doctor if you feel unwell, or if you come into contact with anyone with chickenpox or shingles.

Osteoporosis

If you are taking steroids it is important to protect yourself against osteoporosis; a serious condition which makes you more likely to break bones

DMARDs

Disease-modifying ant-rheumatoid drugs (DMARDs), such as methotrexate or azathioprine, might be given as 'steroid sparing agents' to allow the steroid dose to be reduced in some people who are getting particularly bad side effects.

'One of the hardest lessons I had to learn was that a job doesn't have to be finished in one "go", or even 2 "goes". It used to take me 3 days to do 1 hour's ironing.'

Jean Miller, PMR-GCA Scotland.

Case study

'It can be difficult coming to terms with the ups and downs of the condition. Your concentration goes; you have no stamina. Life can become very difficult especially if the energy levels keep dropping. I was blessed with a husband who has never complained since I took ill, even though he needed a map to find the kitchen. The effect on the immediate family can be considerable too. You look well and nobody can understand why you can't function normally. All these years I've had constant fleeting pains in every part of my body and I get very edgy when I have them behind my eyes, in my ears or in my jaw because of the risk of going blind. And I still have to rest most afternoons.

'It helps if you can accept what you are able to do each day, even if it's only breathing. One of the hardest lessons I had to learn was that a job doesn't have to be finished in one 'go', or even 2 'goes'. It used to take me 3 days to do 1 hour's ironing. Remember that the condition does get better. I'm 76 and can now do 10 minutes' exercise every morning on my mini-trampoline, using my arms and jogging.

Jean Miller, PMR-GCA Scotland.

Diet and exercise

Eat a balanced diet with lots of fresh vegetables and fruit to keep you healthy, as well as oily fish which contains Omega 3 essential fatty acids which help to reduce inflammation.

To reduce the risk of osteoporosis, make sure you get enough calcium and vitamin D in your diet – talk to your doctor about taking a supplement

Aim for 30 minutes of weight-bearing exercise, such as walking, each day. This can be difficult for people with PMR, but doing what you can, will help relieve stiffness.

If you smoke, stop, and try to reduce alcohol intake.

Temporal arteritis

In around 3 out of 100 cases, people with PMR also develop temporal arteritis, or GCA, where some of the blood vessels in the body become inflamed. The blood supply is then reduced to some areas, including the temples (the area of your head diagonally up from your eyes).

With GCA, there is a risk of losing partial or complete vision, which is irreversible; having a stroke or, rarely, losing hearing. GCA can lead to an aneurysm (a bulge in a blood vessel) in a few cases.

Symptoms of GCA

▓ Loss of vision, blurred vision, double vision, or seeing a shadow over your vision.

▓ Severe headaches.

▓ Pain in your jaw when chewing or pain in your tongue when eating.

▓ Tenderness of your scalp (the surface of your head) – for example, it could hurt to brush your hair or touch your head.

'In around 3 out of 100 cases, people with PMR also develop temporal arteritis, or GCA, where some of the blood vessels in the body become inflamed.'

If you get any pain or swelling in your head, or any problems with your vision, or jaw pain, you must contact your doctor straight away. This is because there is a risk of damage to your sight. If treated early, this damage can be prevented by steroid drugs.

If you have GCA, you will have to start with a higher dose of steroids.

You might also need to see an ophthalmologist (an eye specialist).

PMR and other conditions

As many other conditions can sometimes mimic PMR, about 1 in 10 people who start treatment for PMR turn out, over the next few months, to have a different condition. So their diagnosis is changed and they are given treatment for the other condition.

Top tips for managing PMR

- Take your condition seriously and find out as much as you can about it.
- Keep fit and active, which will help prevent osteoporosis. Activity and movement can also help morning stiffness and aching.
- Be careful not to overdo it – learn how much you can do before your symptoms get worse.
- Ask for help when you need it.
- Try to stay positive and get on with your life.
- Go to see your doctor if your symptoms change or get worse.
- Avoid stress.

Summing Up

Polymyalgia rheumatica is a serious condition causing pain and disability, which can have an impact on your quality of life. However, it can be managed successfully with steroids in most cases, and generally PMR disappears after time - although some people might need to stay on a small dose of medication for many years.

While there's no cure for PMR, moves are afoot to improve the accuracy of diagnosis, including a specific blood test, so treatment can be given in the early stages of the disease. Trials are also underway into new types of steroid treatment and steroid-sparing drugs to help manage PMR. The outlook for anyone suffering from PMR is brighter than it would have been a decade ago.

With thanks to John Kirwan, Professor of Rheumatic Diseases at the University of Bristol, for reviewing this chapter, and to PMR-GCA Scotland for their contribution. www.pmrandgca.org.uk

Chapter Six

Fibromyalgia (FM)

Fibromyalgia, also referred to as FM or Fibro, is a common condition affecting over 2% of the UK population - approximately one million people.

The term fibromyalgia derives from 'fibro', for fibrous tissues, 'my', meaning muscles and 'algia', for pain. More people suffer from fibromyalgia than rheumatoid arthritis, and fibro can have more of an impact on their lives than rheumatoid arthritis or osteoporosis.

What is fibromyalgia?

Fibromyalgia is a condition, sometimes referred to as a syndrome, characterised by chronic widespread musculoskeletal pain, involving connective tissues such as muscles, ligaments and tendons. Strictly speaking, fibromyalgia is not an arthritic condition as the joints are usually normal, but it's common in patients with other 'established' rheumatic conditions, such as rheumatoid arthritis and lupus.

There are usually no outward signs of the condition and people with fibro often look well but feel anything but – which can make it difficult for their family and friends to realise the pain and discomfort they're feeling.

Common symptoms

Symptoms tend to come and go, but pain throughout the body is almost universal among those with fibro. The pain might be quite mild some days; at other times so severe sufferers' working, personal and social lives are affected. Some people find that their symptoms are worse in cold or damp weather.

Although painful areas often include the upper back, shoulders and neck, most people with fibromyalgia complain of aching all over their body; sometimes with a burning or throbbing feeling in their muscles. Other symptoms include:

'Fibromyalgia, also referred to as FM or Fibro, is a common condition affecting over 2% of the UK population – approximately one million people.'

Fatigue

This can be mild in some and debilitating in others who feel totally drained of energy.

Depression and anxiety

30% of patients with FM suffer from depression, which usually goes hand-in-hand with feelings of anxiety and an inability to cope with life.

Irritable bowel syndrome (IBS)

Constipation, diarrhoea and frequent abdominal pain are symptoms found in up to two-thirds of cases.

Poor concentration and memory

Sometimes referred to as 'fibro fog'.

Stiffness

Particularly in the morning.

Chronic headaches

Persistent headaches and migraines are common in 50% of cases.

Incontinence

Feeling an urgent need to pass water.

Sleep deprivation

Sleep disorders among fibromyalgia sufferers are common and are thought to be a major contributing factor to the symptoms of the condition.

People with fibro usually fall asleep without too much trouble, but their deep-level sleep can be interrupted by bursts of brain activity, as though they're awake. Being deprived of deep, restorative sleep contributes to people with fibro feeling unmotivated, lacking in energy and ultimately depressed.

Myalgic Encephalomyelitis (ME)

The symptoms common in myalgic encephalomyelitis (also known as ME, or chronic post-viral fatigue) can be similar to those of fibromyalgia, although ME sufferers usually have some kind of viral infection before symptoms appear and don't suffer the pain associated with fibromyalgia. Not enough is known as to whether these two conditions are in fact one and the same.

How is fibromyalgia diagnosed?

There is no specific blood test or X-ray for fibromyalgia, although some tests are made to rule out other rheumatic conditions, such as polymyalgia rheumatica (PMR). Early diagnosis can help in a number of ways, including reducing frustration and preventing muscles getting out of condition.

Tender points

Most of us have tender points across our body. If enough pressure is applied to these points the pressure is uncomfortable, but in fibromyalgia these points can be very tender even if they are pressed gently. If there's tenderness at a number of points – 11 out of a possible 18 - this can help a doctor or rheumatologist make a firm diagnosis of fibro.

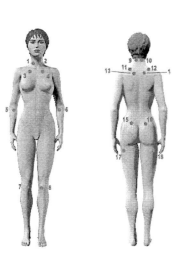

Courtesy of www.UKfibromyalgia.com

'People with fibro usually fall asleep without too much trouble, but their deep-level sleep can be interrupted by bursts of brain activity, as though they're awake.'

Who is likely to be affected?

Fibromyalgia is seven times more common in women than men. The exact reason for this is unknown. Fibromyalgia shows up in people of all ages.

What causes fibromyalgia?

While the actual cause is unknown, there are likely to be a number of factors involved. It's thought fibro is an illness which has both a physical and mental side. The amount of pain felt by someone with fibro is often affected by the way they're feeling, and vice versa.

Sometimes there's no obvious trigger, although the condition often appears after some form of trauma, such as a whiplash injury sustained during a car accident. A viral infection, childbirth and an emotional event, such as a bereavement, can also trigger fibromyalgia.

Recent research has suggested that the nerves responsible for detecting and interpreting pain have become over sensitive. There is believed to be a genetic link.

Is fibromyalgia a condition for life?

FM is a chronic, life-long condition in most sufferers. It causes significant disability and reduces quality of life.

Case study

'I started developing symptoms of fibromyalgia when I was 19 during a year off between college and university. For me, it came on very suddenly with severe pain in my right hip which the doctors could find no explanation for. I was given crutches to help me get around which soon led to me developing pain in my wrists and elbows, followed by pain in my left hip, all completely inexplicable. I saw a range of consultants who were all baffled by my symptoms and in the end decided they must be psychological. At university I developed further symptoms of pain in my jaw, neck, shoulders, knees and terrible insomnia. I ached all over and was permanently tired, to the point of exhaustion.

'This situation carried on for four years with various doctors giving opinions and the pain coming and going over time. Finally I was diagnosed with fibromyalgia and chronic fatigue syndrome by a rheumatologist. However, at that point in the mid-90s, little treatment was on offer and I was told to simply go home and get on with it. I did start taking tricyclic antidepressants to help with the pain, sleeplessness and depression but the medication had a minimal effect.

'As the years went by I tried various medications, went on a pain management course, had physiotherapy and hydrotherapy, found an understanding GP and a superb counsellor. I found painkillers that worked for me and medication that helped me sleep. I still struggle with the symptoms of fibromyalgia but I've reached a point where I know how to pace myself and to manage the symptoms so that I can achieve my goals and gain joy and satisfaction from life again.'

Kathy from the West Midlands.

'I've reached a point where I know how to pace myself and to manage the symptoms so that I can achieve my goals and gain joy and satisfaction from life again.'
Kathy from the West Midlands.

Treatments available

There are a number of medications that can help. More traditional treatments are aimed at improving sleep quality as well as treating depression and reducing muscle pain. These treatments include amitriptyline and dothiepin.

Medicines that boost the body's level of serotonin and noradrenalin –
neurotransmitters that modulate sleep, pain and immune-system function - are
commonly prescribed. Examples of these drugs include sinequan (Doxepin)
and seroxat (Paroxetine). A low dose of these medications can improve sleep
quality and reduce the perception of pain.

Your doctor might prescribe painkillers, such as paracetamol, or a steroid
injection if part of your body is particularly painful. Your might be referred to a
physiotherapist to help you improve your posture and relax your muscles, or a
counsellor to help you adjust to the diagnosis of fibro.

Cognitive behavioural therapy (CBT)

Your GP might be able to refer you for cognitive behavioural therapy – a
psychological treatment based on the assumption that most people's emotional
and behavioural reactions are learned and can be changed. It has been effective
in helping people cope with the pain associated with fibromyalgia.

Top tips for managing fibromyalgia

There are a number of ways you can ease the symptoms of this condition
including:

- Take exercise – low impact forms such as walking and swimming are best.
- Apply heat – a hot water bottle, warm bath or shower will reduce pain and
  morning stiffness.
- Eat a healthy, balanced diet.
- Reduce coffee, tea and alcohol.
- Don't smoke.
- Keep your weight under control.
- Discuss your medication with your doctor if you want to change the
  prescription or switch to another drug.
- Pace yourself - listen to your body if it tells you to slow down and rest.
- Consider complementary therapies to help you relax.

62

Summing Up

Fibromyalgia is a painful condition which can seriously affect the quality of life of those who suffer from the syndrome. However, there are treatments available which can help alleviate some of the symptoms – particularly the pain and fatigue which people feel.

While there's as yet no cure, research into the development of better treatments for fibro sufferers and a greater understanding of this condition means the future is more positive than ever before.

With thanks to Dr Ernest Choy, consultant rheumatologist and member of the Medical Advisory Board of the Fibromyalgia Association UK for his assistance in compiling this chapter and the association for their help with background information. www.fmauk.org

Chapter Seven

Gout

Historically, gout has been seen as something that affects older men who have lived the high life, enjoying rich food and consuming rather a lot of alcohol. Even now, gout is seen as not that serious – almost something to laugh about. Yet anyone who has suffered from this painful condition knows it's no laughing matter.

What is gout?

Gout is a type of arthritis that causes sudden and extremely painful inflammatory attacks in the joints. About one and a half percent of the UK population suffers from gout, and there has been an increase in numbers over the last 30 years.

The condition tends to affect men between the ages of 40 and 60; particularly those who are overweight and genetically predisposed to getting the condition and who have diets high in animal proteins and alcohol. It's less common in men under 30 and pre-menopausal women. Children rarely get gout.

Attacks in women are now on the increase, with twice as many older women now suffering from gout as they did in the 1980s.

The main causes of gout

Gout is caused by excess uric acid in the bloodstream. Most people with gout have high levels of uric acid in their system because it's not efficiently removed by the kidneys and washed out in the urine. It can also be caused by too high levels of uric acid in the diet. The main triggers are:

'Historically, gout has been seen as something that affects older men who have lived the high life, enjoying rich food and consuming rather a lot of alcohol.'

- Lifestyle – including crash dieting.
- Excess weight.
- Stress.
- Prolonged illness.
- Injury.
- Alcohol – particularly beer.
- Some drugs - such as water tablets and aspirin.

Case study

'I've been a heavy drinker for most of my life and even though my doctor and my wife warned me it was harmful and I should cut down, I carried on and suffered attacks of gout on a regular basis. The attacks were very painful; particularly in my big toe. It would throb like mad. One time I couldn't stand, let alone put any weight on my foot, and I was in agony. When my drinking was at its heaviest – strong beer and cider mostly - my gout was at its worst. Then just over a year ago I decided to give up drinking – and my gout attacks stopped. I just wish I'd given up earlier.

'I've also made a lot of changes to my diet at the same time – I eat much more fish than red meat now - so it's no doubt the combined effect of a better diet and less alcohol working for me. My advice would be if you are a heavy drinker, then apart from helping your liver, not having to put up with the pain of gout should be high up on your list of reasons to stop! I've never looked back.'

Simon from Essex.

Genetic link

Much less commonly, people with gout produce too much uric acid in the first place, due to an inherited (genetic) abnormality, or one of the disorders associated with increased production of cells in the body. In around 10% of gout cases there is a family history of the disorder.

What is uric acid?

All of the cells in the human body, and many of the foods we eat, contain substances, or chemical compounds, known as purines. As old cells are broken down or as foods are digested, these purines are converted to uric acid. The pain in gout is caused when the uric acid forms crystals in the joints.

As well as acute joint pain and swelling, high levels of uric acid can cause kidney stones, as well as crystalline lumps along the edge of the ears or over the joints such as the knuckles – known as gouty tophi.

The main symptoms of gout

A sudden, unexpected (acute) attack of gout often develops during the night or in the early hours of the morning. It reaches a peak within a few hours, often making even the touch of bed clothes on the affected joint unbearable.

The skin might be red and shiny and the inflammation might be so severe that the skin peels. A mild fever, loss of appetite and a feeling of tiredness can also accompany acute attacks of gout.

Blood tests to help diagnosis

In terms of diagnosis, a blood test (or multiple blood tests) to measure uric acid levels in the blood will be carried out. Gout is traditionally associated with high plasma uric acid concentration (hyperuricaemia). However, a blood test alone will not prove that an attack of joint pain is due to gout.

A more specific test is the analysis of the fluid in the joint affected. Fluid from the space between the joint is aspirated (removed) and then examined under a microscope. The presence of needle-like uric acid crystals confirms the diagnosis of gout. Other tests include checking the ratio of uric acid to creatinine (chemical waste from muscle) in the urine sample.

'High levels of uric acid can also cause kidney stones.'

Which joints are affected?

Traditionally, the big toe joint is affected, perhaps because it's subjected to such heavy loads and liable to wear and tear. Gout seems to single out a joint that is already in trouble from a degree of damage.

Other joints, such as the knee, ankle, elbow and even the small joints of the hands can be affected too.

Who is likely to develop gout?

Men are much more frequently affected than pre-menopausal women. The cause for this is not entirely clear, but men tend to have higher uric acid levels in their blood after puberty.

In women, there is only a slight gradual increase until the menopause and thereafter levels rise closer to those seen in men. The risk of developing gout increases in line with uric acid levels, but this increase is less marked in post-menopausal women.

Post-menopausal women

The way gout affects the joints in post-menopausal women can also be slightly different. Gout might develop more slowly, particularly affecting joints already showing signs of osteoarthritis.

The marked increase in middle-aged and elderly women getting gout is in part linked to the increasing use of diuretic drugs for the treatment of high blood pressure and heart disease.

More than one attack

An untreated attack generally lasts for a few days, then dies down and the joint gradually returns to normal. Some people never experience another attack. If the uric acid level remains high, most will have a second attack between six months and two years after the first. Untreated attacks will become more frequent and more prolonged.

How is gout treated?

The most important thing is for your doctor to treat the pain and inflammation as soon as possible using painkillers such as non-steroidal anti-inflammatory drugs (NSAIDs), colchicine or steroids.

Once the attack has passed, the next step is to help prevent the attacks returning. If overweight, you might be advised to lose weight slowly, reduce alcohol consumption and eat smaller amounts of purine-rich foods, such as red meat, offal and seafood.

If you are suffering from repeated attacks, long-term treatment to lower the level of uric acid in the blood is usually required. Drugs in this category include:

- Allopurinol, a drug that reduces production of uric acid in the body

- Febuxostat, a new medicine for sufferers who cannot tolerate alluporinol

- Uricosuric drugs which lower urate levels in the blood by increasing the excretion of uric acid in the urine

'An untreated attack generally lasts for a few days, then dies down and the joint gradually returns to normal.'

Top tips for managing gout

There is a three-step approach to managing gout: treating the acute attack; reducing the likelihood of attacks through diet and lifestyle and lowering uric levels to prevent further attacks

During an attack

▓ Ideally, keep off the joint.

▓ Ice packs might ease the swelling and pain of a sudden attack, as will placing the affected joint in a cold bath.

▓ Elevate the joint as much as possible.

Reducing the likelihood of another attack

▓ Drink lots of fluids (e.g. 8-10 glasses of water each day) to prevent dehydration.

▓ If you are overweight, try shedding a few pounds gradually

▓ Avoid crash dieting and fasting as this can lead to uric acid retention by the kidneys

▓ Reduce consumption of alcohol – particularly beer, lager and fortified wines and also sugar sweetened drinks. Never binge drink

▓ Avoid foods rich in purines, particularly red meat, offal and seafood. The UK Gout Society's factsheet *All About Gout and Diet* will tell you more (www.ukgoutsociety.org)

Getting help

If you are worried you might have gout, visit your GP as soon as possible. Your doctor will be able to check whether you have the condition and, if so, prescribe the drug that is most appropriate to relieve the pain and swelling for you. He or she might also refer you to a rheumatologist for further investigation and advice.

Joint damage

If left untreated, gout can lead to joint damage. Untreated attacks will become more frequent and more prolonged and might result in damage to the cartilage and bone.

Summing Up

Gout is a painful condition which mainly affects younger men but women can get it too, particularly after the menopause. Some people have just one attack of gout; others suffer frequent attacks, largely depending on their diet and lifestyle.

By making changes – including avoiding certain foods - and taking the right medication, uric acid levels can be kept below a certain target level in the blood and the chances of your suffering another attack of gout is then reduced considerably, if not completely.

With special thanks to Dr Alastair Hepburn, Consultant Rheumatologist, Worthing Hospital, one of the medical trustees of the UK Gout Society, for his help in compiling this chapter. www.ukgoutsociety.org

Chapter Eight

Arthritis – The Future

An interview with Jane Tadman, Press Officer of Arthritis Research UK, and Professor Alan Silman, Medical Director of Arthritis Research UK on the future for arthritis treatments; the ongoing research into the causes of this disease and hopes for a cure.

Q: Where are we now with treatments for rheumatoid arthritis and other inflammatory arthritic conditions? For example, regarding the latest biologic drugs, how much difference are they making and are they suitable for everyone?

A: The latest biologic drugs, pioneered and developed by Arthritis Research UK scientists, have made an enormous difference to millions of people with inflammatory forms of arthritis around the world. There are currently five in the anti-TNF (tumour necrosis factor) class:

- Infliximab (Remicade).

- Etanercept (Enbrel).

- Adalimumab (Humira).

- Certolizumab pegol (Cimzia).

- Golimumab (Simponi).

All are licensed and all but golimumab are approved by NICE, the National Institute for Health and Clinical Excellence.

'The latest biologic drugs, pioneered and developed by Arthritis Research UK scientists, have made an enormous difference to millions of people with inflammatory forms of arthritis.'

Tocilizumab (RoActemra) blocks an inflammatory pathway called I-I6 and abatacept (Orencia), which also blocks part of the immune pathway, are also licensed for rheumatoid arthritis and other inflammatory types of arthritis.

Another biologic drug, which targets B-cells in the body and works in a slightly different way, called rituximab (Mabthera), is also now available.

These drugs are prescribed for people with severe forms of inflammatory arthritis, and are effective in around 70% of people who take them. Although not a cure, they can dramatically improve symptoms of joint pain and stiffness, and also reduce the extreme fatigue characteristic of rheumatoid arthritis. Increased numbers of new agents gives greater choice.

They are not suitable, appropriate or indeed licensed for people with mild disease, but are given to those in whom conventional treatments such as methotrexate are not working or not tolerated.

They are not prescribed in early disease as a first-line treatment for both clinical and cost reasons.

Q: What are the benefits of 'tight control' in the management of RA? For example, is it fair to say the faster we can switch off the inflammation in RA at every stage of the disease, the better it is for the sufferer?

A: It is important to get inflammatory arthritis under control as quickly as possible to prevent joint damage and slow down disease progression.

Ideally, treatment should start within three months of symptoms appearing, but because of delays in patients accessing a rheumatologist, this doesn't always happen.

Combinations of disease-modifying ant-rheumatoid drugs (DMARDs) such as methotrexate and sulphasalazine can be effective, and ideally patients should be seen regularly by their rheumatology team for doses to be adjusted as needed. Again, this doesn't always happen.

An Arthritis Research UK study from Scotland a few years ago showed that working hard with existing DMARDs to achieve tight control can bring about similar clinical benefits with use of biologics.

Q: Are the causes of arthritis any clearer? Is there a genetic link, for example?

A: There is lots of research in both rheumatoid arthritis and osteoarthritis identifying the role of genes. Not a single gene is involved, and it is likely that multiple genes play a part. Some people are more genetically predisposed to developing both osteoarthritis and rheumatoid arthritis than others.

Nodal osteoarthritis, which particularly affects the hands of middle-aged women, runs strongly in families. And some rare forms of osteoarthritis that start at an earlier age are linked with genes that affect collagen – an essential component of cartilage. Genetic factors play a significant part in knee and hip osteoarthritis, although factors such as obesity and joint injury are also important in these types.

'The so-called "Holy Grail" of most researchers and rheumatologists is to develop "personalised medicine".'

The genes people inherit from their parents may affect the likelihood of developing the disease, but genetic factors alone do not cause rheumatoid arthritis. Even the identical twin of somebody with rheumatoid arthritis, who shares all the same genetic material, only has a 1 in 5 chance of developing the disease. And even where members of the same family have rheumatoid arthritis the severity of the disease can be very different.

There is some evidence that lifestyle factors may affect the risk of developing the disease. For example, rheumatoid arthritis is more common in people who smoke, who eat a lot of red meat or who drink a lot of caffeine. Rheumatoid arthritis is less common in people who have a high vitamin C intake. We still don't understand what triggers rheumatoid arthritis.

There is also an interaction between genes and the environment. For example, smoking has a bigger role in those with susceptible genes.

Rheumatoid arthritis is increased in women especially during their reproductive years, which suggests a hormonal influence. The role of sex hormones is not simple, and complex interaction between hormones may influence disease susceptibility.

Q: How will rheumatoid arthritis be treated in 10 years' time?

A: Within the next decade, more needs to be done to raise awareness among the public and the medical profession of the importance of getting an early diagnosis and treatment, and referral to a rheumatologist. The so-called Holy Grail of most researchers and rheumatologists is to develop 'personalised medicine' so that patients receive the medication that doctors know will best work for them, at the best time, with a greater targeted use of biologics.

The use of biomarkers to choose treatment and assess early response will increase. This may mean prescribing biologic therapy very early in the disease once it has been established that the patient is at risk of developing severe rheumatoid arthritis, but not giving it to patients whose disease is likely to be mild. The aim of clinicians in the future will be to induce remission in early disease, to prevent joint destruction and disease progression.

'How will rheumatoid arthritis be treated in 10 years' time?'

Arthritis Research UK is currently running a clinical trial looking to see if anti-TNF therapy can be tapered down or stopped altogether in patients whose disease is under control, without the return of symptoms.

Q: With osteoarthritis, can you tell us about recent research Arthritis Research UK is carrying out into the causes?

A: Four areas are currently being investigated:

- Genes.
- Biomechanics.
- Inflammation.
- Defects in cartilage repair and regeneration process.

Osteoarthritis is a complex condition affecting both joints and bones, and although many sufferers tend to develop painful symptoms from their 50s upwards, their joints may have been degenerating painlessly much earlier than that. This makes it difficult to research early disease.

Our research is looking at osteoarthritis from many angles: from trying to make everyday life easier for patients by developing better treatments both drug and non-drug; trying to identify the genes that predispose people to developing osteoarthritis, and developing minimally invasive cartilage repair techniques using adult stem cells to prevent the need for joint replacement.

We are also investigating new and novels ways to treat arthritic pain more effectively, as there is a big gap in the market for effective, side effect-free painkillers. Our first three national centres of research excellence looking at primary care research, biomechanics and bioengineering and pain, are all focusing on osteoarthritis.

Q: What is the role of biomarkers in diagnosis – could they really be of major significance?

Biomarkers in the blood will be increasingly used to help make an early or definitive diagnosis, as well as identifying subgroups for treatment choice or treatment response. As mentioned earlier, this is likely to have a significant effect on treatment.

Q: Finally, are we any nearer to finding a cure for arthritis?

A: There is unlikely to be a 'eureka' moment when suddenly a cure for arthritis is found.

Arthritis in its broadest sense is a collection of conditions affecting joints, bones, muscles and connective tissues: osteoarthritis and rheumatoid arthritis are two of the most common, but there is also ankylosing spondylitis, psoriatic arthritis, lupus, osteoporosis, back pain - the list goes on.

In rheumatoid arthritis, biologic therapies will continue to be developed and refined and better targeted; in osteoarthritis the aim is to slow down disease progression by minimally invasive cartilage repair techniques before cartilage has been too badly damaged. If either of these two things can be achieved, we will be well on the way to talking about possible cures, but despite the best efforts of our hundreds of researchers around the UK, that may still be some way off.

Arthritis Research UK is the charity leading the fight against arthritis. It is the only charity in the UK solely dedicated to investigating arthritis in all its forms, and their research programmes are constantly working to discover more about the causes of arthritis and provide better treatment for arthritis sufferers.

Everything they do is underpinned by research. They currently fund more than 350 grants, fellowships and clinical trials in universities and medical schools around the UK, into the causes, treatment and cure of conditions such as rheumatoid arthritis, osteoarthritis, ankylosing spondylitis, lupus, osteoporosis and back pain. www.arthritisresearchuk.org

Chapter Nine

Complementary Therapies

Complementary therapies have never been more popular. For some people they offer a real relief from certain symptoms or the side effects of their conventional treatment. Generally speaking, these therapies are safe if practised by a qualified therapist from a recognised organisation, but always consult your doctor before trying any of them to make sure they're right for you.

What are complementary therapies?

As their name suggests, complementary therapies are designed to be taken alongside conventional medicines and treatments – not replace them. While they seem to help in most cases, these therapies cannot alter the course of the disease or provide a cure, sadly.

Some have been practised for centuries in Egypt, India and China; and while each therapy has a different philosophy, most share a common belief in 'self-healing'.

The power of belief is very strong in health and for some people, the expectation that something will work, makes it work for them.

Holistic approach

While conventional medicine focuses on treating the symptoms of an illness, complementary therapies consider how the whole body is functioning - hence holistic – and take into account people's diet, emotions and lifestyle.

'As their name suggests, complementary therapies are designed to be taken alongside conventional medicines and treatments – not replace them.'

These therapies also encourage people to participate as fully as possible in their own treatment; perhaps by making lifestyle changes, doing more exercise, avoiding stress and adopting a more positive approach to life.

While scientific research on most complementary therapies is relatively new and the studies quite small, early results show that some therapies might help ease physical and emotional symptoms in some people. Each complementary therapy works on different symptoms.

There are too many complementary therapies available in the UK to cover them all in this chapter, but here are some of the more popular ones.

Acupuncture

Acupuncture is rooted in ancient Chinese ideas about how energy moves around the body. The treatment uses fine needles inserted through the skin at specific points to help relieve pain and promote wellbeing in other parts of the body. The needles are usually left in for around twenty minutes. Although it can be slightly uncomfortable as the needles are being inserted, it shouldn't hurt.

The belief is that by the insertion of the needles a message is sent to the spinal column which closes the 'pain gate', blocking pain impulses to the brain. Generally, 3-6 treatments are required, although long-standing complaints might benefit from more sessions.

Acupuncture is safe when practised by a properly qualified therapist (using only disposable needles) and can be useful as a form of pain relief for lower back or knee pain and frozen shoulder (capsulitis). Many acupuncturists will also use acupressure as part of their treatment, using their fingers, thumbs and even feet and knees to stimulate acupoints. To find a practitioner in your area, contact the British Acupuncture Council (www.acupuncture.org.uk).

Alexander Technique

Developed in Australia in the 1890s by actor F Matthias Alexander to improve his voice, this technique concentrates on how we use our bodies in everyday life and teaches people new ways of using the body to improve balance, co-ordination and awareness.

The thinking behind it is by learning to stand and move correctly, muscle tension and poor posture can be prevented. Alexander Technique practitioners prefer to call themselves 'teachers' rather than therapists as they regard what they do as 're-education.'

The Alexander Technique is generally taught one-to-one usually for between 15 and 30 sessions. (www.alexandertrust.org.uk)

Aromatherapy

Aromatherapy combines the benefits of touch with the therapeutic properties of essential oils made from plant extracts. How these oils work is not entirely clear, but users generally respond well to the oils' strong aromas and the absorption of these oils through the skin.

Each oil has its own particular properties – some are stimulating, some relaxing and some act as anti-inflammatories. Rosemary, camomile, marjoram and juniper oils are all thought to be good for muscular or joint aches and pains. As some oils can be toxic, only consult a professional and trained aromatherapist. (www.aromatherapycouncil.co.uk)

Bowen Technique

The Bowen Technique is a soft tissue remedial therapy, named after its innovator Tom Bowen. The technique involves the therapist using their fingers or thumbs to move over muscle, ligaments and tendons in various parts of the body.

'The Bowen Technique is a soft tissue remedial therapy, named after its innovator Tom Bowen. The work is very subtle and gentle.'

The work is very subtle and gentle, involving no hard or prolonged pressure. The treatment can be carried out while the client lies on a therapy table or bed, or sits in a chair. Most of the work can be performed through light clothing, although some therapists prefer to work directly on skin.

Although each session will vary according to the skill and experience of the therapist and the client's symptoms, an initial treatment will consider the body as a whole. Generally, the moves will be made over the lower and mid back and legs, followed by the upper back and shoulders before finishing with neck moves with the client face up. One feature of the work is that between sets of moves the therapist will leave the room and allow the client to rest.

A session will last generally around 45 minutes, and an initial set of three treatments is recommended to establish whether someone is likely to respond to treatment. (www.thebowentechnique.com)

Chiropractic

Devised in Canada in the late 19th century, chiropractic has gained respect from the medical community. The therapy treats problems with joints, bones and muscles and the effects they have on the nervous system. It aims to improve mobility and relieve pain.

'Hydrotherapy allows people with arthritis to exercise their joints and muscles while being supported by warm water.'

Chiropractors use their hands to adjust the joints in the spine and other parts of the body where movement is restricted. While they cannot reverse the damage in joints affected by arthritis, chiropractors claim that this regular adjustment can keep joints healthier and more mobile, while also reducing pain and slowing down further damage. On your first visit, a chiropractor will usually take X-rays of your spine.

Where there's inflammation (during a flare-up of rheumatoid arthritis for example), infection, or signs of osteoporosis, treatment shouldn't be given. (www.chiropractic-uk.co.uk)

Hydrotherapy

Hydrotherapy allows people with arthritis to exercise their joints and muscles while being supported by warm water. The warm temperature of the water helps relax your muscles and ease pain in the joints. As the water supports your weight, the range of movement in your joints should also increase.

You can improve muscle strength by pushing your arms and legs against the water. Most hydrotherapy pools range in depth and have steps to get into the pool but there is normally a hoist available. A physiotherapist oversees the session. You might be referred by your rheumatologist for the therapy (some teaching hospitals have their own hydrotherapy pools), or you could pay for sessions privately. Contact the Chartered Society of Physiotherapists (www.csp.org.uk).

Herbalism

Whereas conventional medicine tries to isolate the active ingredient of a plant, herbal remedies use the whole plant. Herbalists argue that the natural chemical balance in the whole plant has a better effect on the body than giving the patient just the active ingredients.

Herbalism works by stimulating the natural healing processes of the body by rebalancing and cleansing it. Practitioners believe that if correctly prescribed, herbs can be combined and targeted to activate, regulate and heal any organ in the body - unless the tissue has been completely destroyed.

Herbal remedies are popular with some people who believe that they help to cure different forms of rheumatism, and some clinical trials have shown some benefits in relieving symptoms, reducing inflammation and improving mood.

If herbal remedies are going to work, they need to be taken for around 3 months before someone feels the full benefit. They are usually safe but sometimes, like drugs, cause side effects. Contact the National Institute of Medical Herbalists (www.nimh.org.uk).

Massage

Instinctively we use massage to 'rub something better', and as a therapy massage can loosen stiff muscles and ease tension. It can also increase the flow of blood and lymph through the body. An effective massage should leave you feeling relaxed and more positive.

Swedish massage – the most widely available technique in the UK – generally takes place on a special table, and for a full body massage it's usual to undress down to underwear with towels over you. Contact the General Council of Massage Therapy (www.gcmt.org.uk).

Osteopathy

Osteopaths believe that for your body to work well, your bones, muscles, ligaments and tendons must all work together.

To do this, osteopaths use 'adjustments' of the joints (like chiropractors) and more relaxing manipulation in softer areas, to correct structural and mechanical faults and allow the body to heal itself.

Osteopathy is most commonly used for back and joint pain – arthritis, sciatica, frozen shoulders and sports injuries. It should not be used to treat people with osteoporosis, inflamed joints or during the first three months of pregnancy. Many doctors are happy to refer their patients for osteopathy - sometimes on the NHS. (www.osteopathy.org)

Reflexology

Reflexologists believe that stimulating specific parts of your feet can help remove energy blocks - relieving stress and allowing the body to heal itself. Their view is that pressure applied to one part of the body, using a finger or thumb, can relieve pain in another part.

While reflexology is generally relaxing, it can be painful on a sensitive reflex point. Reflexology is not as well regulated as it could be, but to become a member of the Association of Reflexologists, therapists must have a recognised qualification, one year's experience and a number of successful case histories under their belt. Contact the Association of Reflexologists (www.aor.org.uk).

Homeopathy

Medical homeopaths are doctors (or other health professionals) who have additional qualifications in homeopathy. Non-medical homeopaths are professionals who only practise homeopathy.

Homeopathy is based on the principle of 'like is cured by like'. Where conventional medicine aims to suppress symptoms - for example by using anti-inflammatories to reduce inflammation - homeopathy provokes the body into healing itself.

Homeopathic remedies can come from vegetables or minerals – and sometimes animals. Although some are potentially toxic they are used in such a diluted form that there is usually no danger. Side effects are unusual, and remedies are not normally harmful when taken alongside conventional medicines but always check with your doctor first. (www.britishhomeopathic.org)

Top tips on complementary therapies

- Always check with your GP before embarking on any complementary therapies and ask if you could be referred on the NHS.

- Make sure your therapist is a member of a professional body. The Complementary and Natural Healthcare Council (CNHC) is the UK regulatory body. Contact them to find a therapist (www.cnhc.org.uk).

- Ask your therapist how long the treatment will take and how much it will cost.

- Check with your GP before stopping any prescribed drugs, and beware of any therapist suggesting you do so without your GP's consent.

- Weigh up the benefits of complementary therapies against any possible side effects.

'Always check with your GP before embarking on any complementary therapies and ask if you could be referred on the NHS.'

Summing Up

Complementary therapies can be effective in helping to relieve symptoms such as pain and stiffness, and to help you relax. They can also help psychologically by making you feel you're doing your bit to help manage your condition.

These therapies are designed to work alongside conventional treatments, not replace them, so never stop taking your conventional treatment without your GP's consent. And always check with your doctor before embarking on a new therapy as some might be more suitable for your condition than others.

With thanks to Arthritis Care www.arthritiscare.org.uk and Arthritis Research UK www.arthritisresearchuk.org for their help in compiling this chapter.

Chapter Ten

Diet and Exercise

Eating a balanced diet, keeping hydrated and building exercise into your daily routine not only improves your general health, but helps relieve the pain and stiffness associated with arthritis. And it's easier than you think to lead a healthy lifestyle. With a little effort, it could become almost second nature.

Importance of a balanced diet

Most people know that it's important to eat a balanced diet and avoid processed foods high in saturated fat and sugar. According to NHS guidelines (www.nhs.uk/livewell) carbohydrates should make up about one-third of our daily diet; fruit and vegetables another third and the remainder should be split between protein and milk and dairy. By following a healthy, balanced diet, you should be getting the right amount of vitamins and minerals you need to stay healthy.

Fatty acids

Whether what you eat can have an effect on your arthritis isn't clear, but studies on essential fatty acids called Omega 3s (found naturally in oily fish) show that they can ease joint pain and stiffness – though it might take several months to feel the full benefits. Try to include more Omega 3-rich foods in your diet and consider taking a supplement.

As Omega 3 fats can lead to the production of harmful substances called free radicals, it's important to eat these fats alongside plenty of antioxidants (found in brightly coloured fruits and vegetables) including vitamin E (found in sweet potatoes, avocados and nuts/seeds).

'Whether what you eat can have an effect on your arthritis isn't clear, but studies on essential fatty acids called Omega 3s (found naturally in oily fish) show that they can ease joint pain and stiffness.'

A healthy diet should include a balance between Omega 3 and Omega 6 fatty acids. Most people have enough Omega 6 fatty acids in their diet (found in meat such as pork and turkey) and usually don't need to add any. If in doubt, check with a dietician.

Flare-ups

Some people notice that certain foods make their arthritis flare up. (This is when the inflammation is more active and the swelling and stiffness worse). If you notice this, and can work out which food is to blame, it makes sense to cut it out of your diet - as long as you don't miss out on essential nutrients in the process.

'People with rheumatoid arthritis are at increased risk of developing osteoporosis, so ensuring an adequate calcium intake is very important.'

Essential minerals

It's not only vitamins such as C, E and various B vitamins that are important for good health; certain minerals are essential to keeping us fit and well too – and could even prevent arthritis developing in the first place. These include:

Calcium with Vitamin D

People with rheumatoid arthritis are at increased risk of developing osteoporosis, so ensuring an adequate calcium intake is very important.

Foods rich in calcium include sardines, milk, yoghurt, cheese and green leafy vegetables such as cabbage.

Vitamin D is also needed for the body to absorb calcium. The main source of vitamin D is from sunlight on our skin, but it is also found in oily fish. As we age, we are prone to low levels of vitamin D because of the body's reduced ability to produce the vitamin in this way. As the deficiency is unlikely to be compensated by food, you could take a supplement. Research has shown taking this supplement improves muscle as well as bone strength, and reduces the likelihood of falls in older people.

Magnesium

Magnesium is another important mineral and there have been studies to suggest a lack of magnesium can contribute to the development of arthritis. Foods rich in magnesium include salmon, bananas, spinach, sardines and apples. Herbs and spices, including dill and cumin, are also good sources. Magnesium can help your body absorb calcium and maintain a proper balance between the two minerals.

Some people find adding a few cups of Epsom salts (magnesium sulphate) to their bath or foot soak can help reduce swelling and relax muscles. The salts are available from chemists and health food stores.

Iron

Fatigue is a common symptom of rheumatoid arthritis and can be made worse by anaemia (a deficiency of red blood cells). Anaemia can develop as a result of inflammation, or because of the long-term use of NSAIDs (non-steroidal anti-inflammatories). Also, some people don't get enough iron in their diet. Iron-rich foods include red meat, eggs and fortified breakfast cereals. Iron is more easily absorbed by your body if you have it at the same time as vitamin C, so have a portion of fruit or vegetables with your meal, or perhaps a glass of orange juice.

Reducing inflammation – foods that can help

Certain foods could help people with inflammatory arthritis manage their symptoms. These include:

Berries

Blueberries, blackberries, blackcurrants, cranberries, raspberries and strawberries contain antioxidants that can reduce inflammation. They also contain fibre, folic acid, vitamin C and potassium. Cherries might help reduce pain.

Citrus fruits

Oranges, lemons, limes, kiwis and grapefruit are rich in vitamin C, which might help protect against developing inflammatory arthritis. They also contain fibre, folic acid and potassium.

Vegetables

Broccoli, cauliflower, cabbage and Brussels sprouts are good for the heart, and as people with rheumatoid arthritis are at increased risk of developing heart disease, eating sufficient quantities of these vegetables is important.

Ongoing laboratory research has found that a compound in broccoli called sulforaphane blocks the enzymes that cause damage to joints in osteoarthritis; and high amounts of garlic also appear to slow the destruction of cartilage.

Apple cider vinegar

Some people believe that apple cider vinegar (converted from acid to alkaline in the body) and often taken with honey, will help relieve stiffness and even cure arthritis, yet there is no scientific evidence for this.

Aloe vera

Aloe can be taken as a drink or applied externally as a gel. Recent studies on animals into aloe's potential to reduce inflammation are encouraging, although not enough research has been done into its safety. Drinking aloe might alter the effects of prescribed drugs, including steroids, so check with your doctor first.

Bromelain

Bromelain, also known as ananas comosus, is a mixture of protein-digesting enzymes taken from the stem of pineapples. Although claims have been made that it can reduce swelling and pain, there's no real proof as yet. If you're taking antibiotics or blood-thinning medication, such as aspirin or warfarin, you must consult your doctor before taking bromelain as the combination might cause bleeding.

Alcohol

A recent study found that moderate drinking might ease the pain and even lower the risk of developing rheumatoid arthritis. (Alcohol can suppress the immune system). There have also been studies to show that a small glass of beer (real ale) a day can help maintain bone mass. Beer is a good source of folate, magnesium, potassium and niacin.

Always check with your doctor before drinking alcohol, particularly if you are taking some prescribed treatments such as methotrexate, which can cause liver damage if taken with alcohol. Some over-the-counter medicines should not be taken with alcohol either, so always check with a pharmacist.

Supplements

As already mentioned, Omega 3 and vitamin D supplements can be worth taking, and some people find other supplements can help relieve some of the symptoms of their arthritis.

However, certain supplements might react with prescribed drugs and can be dangerous if taken in high doses, so always check with your doctor before taking any.

'A recent study found that moderate drinking might ease the pain and even lower the risk of developing rheumatoid arthritis.'

Popular supplements include:

Evening primrose oil

Evening primrose oil contains the fatty acid gamma-linolenic acid (GLA). Several studies have shown that GLA supplements can relieve inflammation and rheumatoid arthritis. EPO needs to be taken for at least 3 months to feel the benefit; and it might be worth taking it alongside fish oils.

St John's wort

This is a popular herbal remedy derived from a flower, and appears to act as a mild antidepressant by raising serotonin levels – low in people with fibromyalgia. It must be taken for a number of weeks to feel any real effect. As St John's Wort can interfere with some prescribed medicines, check with your doctor before taking it.

Glucosamine sulphate and chondroitin

These supplements can be bought from chemists or health food shops and are sometimes sold as combined tablets. Joint cartilage usually contains glucosamine and chondroitin compounds, and taking supplements of these natural ingredients might help improve the health of damaged cartilage. While there is no scientific evidence of benefit, some people with osteoarthritis think it does them good, and most surgeons and doctors seem to be of the view 'if it works for you, take it'.

Litozin

Litozin is a food supplement derived from wild rose hip and hailed by some as a magic ingredient to beat the pain of osteoarthritis. In some cases it has a positive effect on rheumatoid arthritis too. Some rheumatologists are now recommending Litozin to their patients.

Rosehips and their seeds contain an antioxidant that has an anti-inflammatory effect. Research has shown that the effectiveness of Litozin is likely to stem from GOPO, a fatty acid.

Exercise

Regular exercise should help you to live an independent and more pain-free life. Benefits of exercise include a better range of movement and joint mobility; increased muscle tone and strength and stronger bones. Exercise also helps us keep our weight in check.

Always exercise safely, avoiding high-impact exercise such as jogging or running, and if an exercise hurts, especially in the joint itself, stop immediately. Make sure you drink enough water and check with your doctor or physiotherapist before starting any new exercise regime.

Types of exercise

A good exercise programme for people with arthritis includes strengthening muscles which protect and support the joints, and aerobic exercise which helps maintain a strong heart.

You should warm up by doing gentle exercises first and cool down after stopping. It's important to keep exercising during a flare-up, but gently.

Walking

Although walking doesn't suit everyone with arthritis, it's a good way to strengthen the heart and lungs, as well as the muscles around the hips and knees. Walking is such an easy form of exercise because it can be woven into everyday life – walking to the shops or to work, among other things.

'Although walking doesn't suit everyone with arthritis, it's a good way to strengthen the heart and lungs, as well as the muscles around the hips and knees.'

Swimming

Swimming is a good all-round aerobic exercise for virtually everyone as it stretches and strengthens most muscles, including those in the lungs, as well as giving the heart a good workout. As people can move more freely in the water, it's suited to people with arthritis – water supports the weight of the body, putting minimal strain on joints. Some people with more severe arthritis are referred for hydrotherapy courses where exercise is done in a pool heated to the temperature of a bath under the supervision of a physiotherapist. Ask your rheumatologist or doctor if you might be eligible for hydrotherapy. (Some of the larger hospitals have their own hydrotherapy pool.)

'The results of the first comprehensive analysis of tai chi suggest it can reduce pain symptoms and improve disability among arthritis sufferers.'

Dancing

Dancing improves posture, breathing and general fitness and is fun and sociable, so you are more likely to stick with it.

Tai Chi

Performed daily by millions of Chinese people, tai chi aims to improve the flow of chi (energy), calm the mind and promote self-healing. Tai chi uses sequences of slow, graceful movements and it's best to learn these moves in classes where the teacher can correct your posture. The results of the first comprehensive analysis of tai chi suggest it can reduce pain symptoms and improve disability among arthritis sufferers. (Tai Chi Union for Great Britain: www.taichiunion.com)

Yoga

From the Sanskrit word for union between mind, body and spirit, yoga can be practised by people of all ages and abilities. The most widely taught form in the UK is atha yoga to stretch and flex the body; develop breath awareness and promote relaxation. Meditation is sometimes included. Yoga can improve posture, muscle tone and mobility. (The British Wheel of Yoga: www.bwy.org.uk)

Top tips on diet and exercise

- Always eat a balanced diet with lots of fruit and vegetables and cut down on saturated fat and sugar.

- Never start taking supplements without talking to your doctor first as some can be dangerous in high doses and cause side effects.

- If you feel you need help with dietary choices ask your doctor for advice or consider talking to a dietician.

- If you think you might be deficient in vitamins or minerals, ask to be tested.

- Beware of diets that claim to cure rheumatoid arthritis, and never begin a diet that involves stopping medication without discussing it with your doctor.

- Take regular exercise to keep mobile and strengthen your joints.

- Include exercise you enjoy in your daily routine so it becomes easier to maintain.

- Always consult your doctor or a physiotherapist before embarking on a new exercise programme.

- If any exercise is painful, stop immediately.

Summing Up

It's important to maintain a healthy lifestyle when you have arthritis. This will help you manage your symptoms and stop your arthritis getting worse. By eating a varied diet, keeping hydrated and taking enough exercise, you should be able to enjoy generally good health into the bargain.

It is also important not to get too anxious about what you eat, or fret about the occasional treat. A little bit of what you fancy will probably do you good! If you apply the healthy options rule most of the time then you're likely to be right on track.

With thanks to Arthritis Care www.arthritiscare.org.uk for their help in compiling this chapter.

Help List

Arthritis Care

18 Stephenson Way, London, NW1 2HD
Tel: 0808 800 4050 (helpline)
www.arthritiscare.org.uk
Arthritis Care exists to support people with arthritis. It's the UK's largest charity working with, and for, all people who have arthritis, offering support throughout the UK.

Arthritis and Musculoskeletal Alliance (ARMA)

Bride House, 18-20 Bride Lane, London, EC4Y 8EE
Tel: 0207 842 0910
www.arma.uk.net

The umbrella body providing a collective voice for the arthritis and musculoskeletal community in the UK.

Arthritis Research UK

Copeman House, St Mary's Gate, Chesterfield, Derbyshire, S41 7TD
Tel: 0300 790 0400 (helpline)
www.arthritisresearchuk.org
The charity is leading the fight against arthritis, funding high class research, providing information and campaigning. The charity has been funding the research and treatment of arthritis for 70 years.

British Society for Rheumatology (BSR)

Tel: 0207 842 0900
www.rheumatology.org.uk
BSR promotes excellence in the treatment of people with arthritis and musculoskeletal conditions and supports those delivering it. They have a 25 year history of promoting high quality standards of care and providing education,

training and support to those working in rheumatology. While they are unable to provide medical advice or recommend individual practitioners, they have a list of support groups and reports available to view on their website.

British Orthopaedic Association

35-43 Lincoln's Inn Fields, London, WC2A 3PE
Tel: 0207 405 6507
www.boa.ac.uk
A professional association, with a patient liaison group comprising of orthopaedic surgeons and lay members, and useful publications to download from their website.

Fibromyalgia Association UK

PO Box 206, Stourbridge, West Midlands DY9 8YL
Tel: 0844 887 2444 (helpline)
www.fmauk.org
The Fibromyalgia Association UK is a registered charity dedicated to raising awareness of this condition and to offering support to sufferers and their carers.

Fibro Action

46 The Nightingales, Newbury, RG14 7UJ
Tel: 0844 443 5422
www.fibroaction.org
A charity taking a positive and proactive approach to fibromyalgia syndrome.

Lupus UK

St James House, Eastern Road, Romford, Essex, RM1 3NH
Tel: 01708 731251
www.lupusuk.org.uk
The only national registered charity supporting people with systemic lupus and discoid lupus, and those approaching diagnosis.

National Ankylosing Spondylitis Society (NASS)

Unit 0.2, One Victoria Villas, Richmond, Surrey, TW9 2GW
T: 0208 948 9117
www.nass.co.uk
The only registered charity in the UK working for people with ankylosing spondylitis and their families.

National Osteoporosis Society

Camerton, Bath, BA2 0PJ
Helpline: 0845 450 0230
www.nos.org.uk
The only UK-wide charity dedicated to improving the diagnosis, prevention and treatment of osteoporosis.

National Rheumatoid Arthritis Society (NRAS)

Unit B4 Westacott Business Centre, Westacott Way, Littlewick Green, SL6 3RT
Tel: 0800 298 7650 (helpline)
www.nras.org.uk
NRAS is the only patient-led UK charity specifically for people with rheumatoid arthritis. It provides support for people with RA and produces a range of publications on living with RA, including managing pain, benefits and employment guides for both employees and employers.

Polymyalgia Rheumatica and GCA Scotland

Tel: 01382 562974 (helpline)
www.pmrandgca.org.uk
A charity raising awareness of the condition.

Psoriasis and Psoriatic Arthritis Alliance (PAPAA)

PO Box 111, St Albans, Hertfordshire, AL2 3JQ
Phone: 01923 672837
www.papaa.org.uk
A charity dedicated to helping people affected by psoriasis and psoriatic conditions.

Royal National Hospital For Rheumatic Diseases

Upper Borough Walls, Bath, Somerset, BAI IRL

Tel: 01225 465941

www.rnhrd.nhs.uk

Provides general and specialist rheumatology services and specialist clinics covering connective tissue disease, osteoporosis and ankylosing spondylitis conditions, among others.

St Thomas' Lupus Trust

The Louise Coote Lupus Unit, Gassiot House, St Thomas' Hospital, London, SE1 7EH

www.lupus.org.uk

Runs the biggest lupus unit in Europe and trains doctors from all over the world at the unit. The unit takes referrals from all over the UK

UK Fibromyalgia.com

www.ukfibromyalgia.com

A website with information and forums. Produces *Family* magazine.

UK Gout Society

PO Box 527, London, WC1V 7YP

www.ukgoutsociety.org

A national charity dedicated to raising public awareness of gout.

Complementary Therapies

British Complementary Medicine Association (BCMA)

PO Box 5122, Bournemouth, BH8 0WG

Tel: 0845 345 5977

www.bcma.co.uk

An umbrella group that maintains a register of qualified practitioners.

British Massage Therapy Council

Cowley, Oxford, OX4 3JU
Tel: 01865 774123
www.bmtc.co.uk
Helps you find a practitioner.

British Osteopathic Association

3 Park Terrace, Manor Road, Luton, LU1 3HN
Tel: 01582 488455
www.osteopathy.org
Helps you find an osteopath near you.

Chartered Society of Physiotherapists

Tel: 020 7306 6666
www.csp.org.uk
Can help you find a chartered physiotherapist who offers private services as
well as hydrotherapists.

College of Occupational Therapists

Tel: 020 7357 6480
www.cot.org.uk
Can help you find an occupational therapist near to where you live.

European College of Bowen Studies

Tel: 01373 832340
www.thebowentechnique.com
A source of information on the technique. Offers assistance in finding a
therapist.

Homeopathic Medical Association

7 Darnley Road, Gravesend, Kent, DA11 ORU
Tel: 01474 560336
www.the-hma.org
Represents qualified professional homeopaths and promotes homeopathy and
homeopathic education. Has a register of homeopaths.

Institute for Complementary and Natural Medicine (ICNM)

Can-Mezzanine, 32-36 Loman Street, London, SE1 0EH
Tel: 0207 922 7980
www.icnm.org.uk
Provides information on all aspects of the safe and best practice of complementary medicine. The institute can also help you find locally qualified practitioners.

International Federation of Professional Aromatherapists

IFPA House, 82 Ashby Rd, Hinkley, Leicestershire LE10 1SN
Tel: 01455 637987
www.ifparoma.org
Maintains a register of practising members whose services are available to the public and professional organisations.

Society of Podiatrists and Chiropodists

1 Fellmonger's Path, Tower Bridge Road, London, SE1 3LY
Tel: 0207 234 8620
www.scpod.org
Professional body for registered podiatrists and chiropodists. Can help you find one in your area.

The Arthritic Association

First Floor Suite, 2 Hyde Gardens, Eastbourne, BN21 4PN
Tel freephone: 0800 652 3188
www.arthriticassociation.org.uk
Aims to relieve the suffering and pain of arthritis by natural methods. Provides dietary guidance with homoeopathic and herbal treatment.

The British Acupuncture Council

Tel: 0208 735 0400
www.acupuncture.org.uk
Contact them to find a practitioner in your area.

The British Chiropractic Association

Tel: 0118 950 5950

www.chiropractic-uk.co.uk

Offers information and assistance in finding a chiropractor in your area.

The British Medical Acupuncture Society (BMAS)

BMAS House, 3 Winnington Court, Northwich, Cheshire, CW8 1AQ

Tel: 01606 786782

Email: admin@medicalacupuncture. org.uk

www.medical-acupuncture.co.uk

A registered charity established to encourage the use of scientific understanding of acupuncture within medicine for public benefit. It seeks to enhance the education and training of suitably qualified practitioners and to promote high standards of working practices in acupuncture.

The Homeopathy Action Trust

15 Clerkenwell Close, London, EC1R 0AA

0844 800 2840

www.homeopathyactiontrust.org

A charity aiming to support and make accessible the art, science and practice of homeopathy, and raise awareness among the public about obtaining real choices for their health needs.

The Society of Teachers of the Alexander Technique

1st floor, Linton House, 39-51 Highgate Road, London, NW5 1RS

Tel: 0207 482 5135

www.stat.org.uk

Has a directory of teachers of the Alexander Technique. The technique aims to improve posture.

Disability Information

Canine Partners

Mill Lane, Heyshot, Midhurst, West Sussex, GU29 OED
Tel: 08456 580 480
www.caninepartners.co.uk
Canine partners transforms the lives of people with disabilities, allowing them to live more independently by partnering them with highly-trained assistance dogs. Training is tailor-made to the needs of the individual. A number of their clients have RA.

Dial UK

Tel: 01302 310123
www.dialuk.org.uk
A charity supplying details of your nearest disability centre and offering advice and an information service.

Disability Rights Handbook

Telephone: 020 7247 8776
www.disabilityalliance.org
Gives more details on DLA and other social security benefits for disabled people, their families and carers. There is a section devoted to the appeals process should your claim be unsuccessful.

Disabled Living Foundation

Helpline: 0845 130 9177
www.dlf.org.uk
The foundation offers advice and information on equipment.

Motability

Tel: 0845 456 4566
www.motability.co.uk
Provides cars and powered wheelchairs through the Motability Scheme.

UK Disabled People's Council (UKDPC)

Stratford Advice Arcade, 107-109 The Grove, Stratford, E15 1HP
Tel: 020 8522 7433
www.ukdpc.net
Campaigns for the rights of disabled people

Benefits Enquiry Line

Helpline: 0800 882200. Monday-Friday 8.30am-6.30pm; Saturday 9am-1pm
Confidential advice and information provided by the Department for Work and
Pensions for people with disabilities, their carers and representatives, about
social security benefits and how to claim them. They also offer assistance with
completing claim forms.

Citizens Advice Bureau (CAB)

www.citizensadvice.org.uk
Offers help with welfare rights, housing and disability advice. Local CABs are
listed in the telephone directory and on their website.

Pain Management

The British Pain Society

Tel: 020 7269 7840
www.britishpainsociety.org
Offers information about pain clinics.

Pain Concern

Tel: 01875 614537
www.painconcern.org.uk
Offers information and a helpline.

Children With Arthritis

The Source

Tel: 0808 808 2000 (10am-4pm weekdays).
Email: theSource@arthritiscare.org.uk
Around 12,000 children in the UK under the age of 16 have a form of arthritis. Most types of childhood arthritis come under the general heading of juvenile idiopathic arthritis (JIA). Arthritis Care has a number of factsheets which can be viewed on their website. It also runs The Source, which offers confidential support for young people, and the parents and families of children with arthritis. You can ring The Source if you are a young person with any questions about arthritis and how it affects your life; or if you are a parent, carer or teacher.

Children's Chronic Arthritis Association

Tel: 01905 745595
www.ccaa.org.uk
Offers support for children with arthritis, and their families.

Health Services

NHS Direct

Tel: 0845 4647
www.nhsdirect.nhs.uk
Can provide information on conditions, treatments, support groups and local NHS services.
In Scotland call NHS 24 Tel: 08454 24 24 24.

Information on Drugs

Medicines and Healthcare Products Regulatory Agency (MHRA)

151 Buckingham Palace Road, London, SW1W 9SZ
Tel: 020 3080 6000
www.mhra.gov.uk
Can provide information on medicines available in the UK on prescription.

Glossary

Anti-DNA
A blood test used to see if antibodies are present to help diagnose conditions such as lupus.

Biologics
Latest treatment for severe forms of inflammatory arthritis. These drugs include anti-TNFs which block the action of a chemical called tumour necrosis factor.

CCP
Cyclic citrullinated reptide antibody - a more modern test for rheumatoid arthritis.

Chiropodists and podiatrists
Treat foot problems and can provide advice on shoes and insoles.

Cox-2 Inhibitors
A newer type of NSAID designed to be gentler on the stomach.

CRP
C-reactive protein – a blood test to check inflammation levels.

DEXA (DXA)
A scan to check the 'density' of bones to help diagnose osteoporosis. Stands for dual energy X-ray absorptiometry.

Dieticians
Can offer advice on eating healthily and can suggest changes to your diet if needed.

DMARDs
Disease modifying ant-rheumatoid drugs. Help tackle the underlying disease.

ESR
Erythrocyte sedimentation rate – a blood test to check levels of inflammation.

MRI scan
Stands for magnetic resonance imaging. This scan uses strong magnetic fields to take pictures of joints and connective tissues. Often used alongside X-rays

NICE
National Institute for Health and Clinical Excellence.

NSAIDs
Non-steroidal anti-inflammatory drugs.

Occupational therapists
Give advice on how to make the most efficient use of your joints without causing anymore damage.

Orthopaedic surgeons
Operate on joints and bones to correct deformities, injuries and general musculoskeletal problems.

Physiotherapists
Can suggest and prepare exercises to keep your muscles strong and to maintain as much movement as possible in your joints.

Rheumatologists
Doctors specialising in inflammatory arthritic conditions. Work within hospital rheumatology departments.

Rheumatology nurses
Nurses who specialise in rheumatology and often hold clinics within hospital rheumatology departments.

Steroids
Also called glucocorticoids or corticosteroids given as drugs or injections to reduce inflammation quickly.

Ultrasound
Uses sound waves to create images and check for joint damage and swelling.

Need - 2 - Know

Need –2– Know

Available Titles Include ...

Allergies A Parent's Guide
ISBN 978-1-86144-064-8 £8.99

Autism A Parent's Guide
ISBN 978-1-86144-069-3 £8.99

Blood Pressure The Essential Guide
ISBN 978-1-86144-067-9 £8.99

Dyslexia and Other Learning Difficulties
A Parent's Guide ISBN 978-1-86144-042-6 £8.99

Bullying A Parent's Guide
ISBN 978-1-86144-044-0 £8.99

Epilepsy The Essential Guide
ISBN 978-1-86144-063-1 £8.99

Your First Pregnancy The Essential Guide
ISBN 978-1-86144-066-2 £8.99

Gap Years The Essential Guide
ISBN 978-1-86144-079-2 £8.99

Secondary School A Parent's Guide
ISBN 978-1-86144-093-8 £9.99

Primary School A Parent's Guide
ISBN 978-1-86144-088-4 £9.99

Applying to University The Essential Guide
ISBN 978-1-86144-052-5 £8.99

ADHD The Essential Guide
ISBN 978-1-86144-060-0 £8.99

Student Cookbook – Healthy Eating The Essential Guide
ISBN 978-1-86144-069-3 £8.99

Multiple Sclerosis The Essential Guide
ISBN 978-1-86144-086-0 £8.99

Coeliac Disease The Essential Guide
ISBN 978-1-86144-087-7 £9.99

Special Educational Needs A Parent's Guide
ISBN 978-1-86144-116-4 £9.99

The Pill An Essential Guide
ISBN 978-1-86144-058-7 £8.99

University A Survival Guide
ISBN 978-1-86144-072-3 £8.99

View the full range at **www.need2knowbooks.co.uk**.
To order our titles call **01733 898103**, email **sales@ n2kbooks.com** or visit the website. Selected ebooks available online.

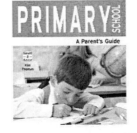

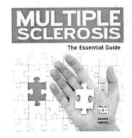

Need - 2 - Know, Remus House, Coltsfoot Drive, Peterborough, PE2 9BF